The **Happy Brain Journal:** The Most Powerful Way to Manifest, Feel Motivated and Improve Self-Esteem

YOUR SUPPORT MAKES A BIG DIFFERENCE!

When you support our business, you're supporting a dream coming to life.

Share a picture or video of your Happy Brain Journal on social media for **20% OFF your next purchase!**

Email hello@quantummindframe.com with your social media post link to receive your special discount.

Let's connect!

Follow our @quantummindframe social channels.

Tools for tapping into your *hidden strengths* and creating positive change in your life.

QUANTUM
MINDFRAME

quantummindframe.com

If found, please contact:

_____
_____

Quantum Mindframe

GET IN TOUCH
hello@quantummindframe.com

CREATED BY
Esma Verma

© 2024 Happy Brain Journal
All rights reserved.

No portion of this book may be reproduced in any form without permission from the publisher, except as permitted by U.S. copyright law.

Happy Brain Journal is owned by Quantum Mindframe

quantummindframe.com

DISCLAIMER

By viewing or using this book, you agree to accept all parts of this Disclaimer. Thus, if you do not agree to the Disclaimer below, STOP now and do not use this book. The information provided in or through this book is for educational and informational purposes only and solely as a self-help tool for your own use. Although I am a psychotherapist, this book is not intended to provide mental health treatment and does not constitute a client/therapist relationship, which is only established after an initial consult and signed consent. I do not, nor do I claim to provide therapy through this book. The information provided in this book is not a replacement for the therapeutic relationship in psychotherapy or the coaching relationship. The information in this book is not intended to replace medical advice. The ideas, procedures, and suggestions outlined in this book are not intended as a substitute for consulting with your physician. The author shall not be liable or responsible for any loss or damage arising from any suggestion or information in this book. You agree that the information in this book is not legal or financial advice. You acknowledge that you are participating voluntarily in using this book and that you are solely and personally responsible for your choices, actions, and results, now and in the future. You accept full responsibility for the consequences of your use, or non-use, of any information provided on or through this book, and you agree to use your own judgment and due diligence before implementing any idea, suggestion, or recommendation from this book to your life, family or business. I cannot predict, and I do not guarantee that you will attain a particular result, and you accept and understand that results differ for each individual. Each individual's results depend on their unique background, dedication, desire, motivation, actions, and numerous other factors. You fully agree that there are no guarantees about the specific outcome or results you can expect from using the information you receive on or through this book. Although every effort has been made to ensure the accuracy of information shared on or through this book, the information may inadvertently contain inaccuracies or typographical errors. You agree that I am not responsible for the views, opinions, or accuracy of facts referenced on or through this book or of those of any other individual or company affiliated with my book or me in any way. Because scientific, technology and business practices are continually evolving, you agree that I am not responsible for this book's accuracy or for any errors or omissions that may occur. Under no circumstances is the author liable or responsible for any losses, direct or indirect, that are incurred due to the use of the information contained within this book, including but not limited to errors, omissions, or inaccuracies. Please consult a licensed professional before attempting any techniques outlined in this book.

Accept no one's definition of your life; define yourself.

HARVEY FIERSTEIN

Contents

Five reasons you will love The Happy Brain Journal 1

How it Works 6

The Tools 12

Journal Entry Examples 18

FAQ 25

The Journal 33

Emotions Glossary 223

How to Feel Your Emotions 228

Vocabulary for Physical Sensations 232

Closing Thoughts 235

Resources 237

Five Reasons You Will Love The Happy Brain Journal

1. IT'S THE MOST POWERFUL WAY TO MANIFEST.

The Happy Brain Journal is designed to train your brain to create a desired state and facilitate reaching your goals. The subconscious mind processes imagination similarly to reality. When we visualize something happening in our minds, our brain and body are responding almost as though that experience is real. Visualizing your goals and desired future has been shown to increase motivation, improve mood, build confidence, and increase the likelihood of achieving those goals.

The secret to manifesting entails three highly refined skills:
- Feeling the positive emotions associated with the expected result of your desired manifestation.
- Maintaining a general positive outlook about life and an internal felt sense of safety through emotional regulation.
- Taking consistent small steps toward reaching your goals.

What you hold your focused attention on is amplified and informs your experience. Holding a focused attention on a desired outcome primes your brain to notice opportunities that can get you to that goal.

Deliberate use of visualization techniques has been shown to build new neural pathways in the brain. The world's top athletes have been using visualization techniques for years. It's time you took advantage of this powerful tool.

The art of manifestation takes practice and highly evolved skill. The Happy Brain Journal is the most powerful way to manifest as it trains your brain and nervous system and helps you stay consistent in your daily practice.

2. IT'S BUILT USING PROVEN PSYCHOLOGY.

The Happy Brain Journal uses components from positive psychology, somatic practices, self-compassion, and experiential therapy, as well as the following evidence-based practices:

Dialectical Behavioral Therapy (DBT)
Acceptance and Commitment Therapy (ACT)

3. IT'S DESIGNED TO TEACH YOUR BRAIN PSYCHOLOGICAL FLEXIBILITY.

Research shows that psychological flexibility can help reduce stress, anxiety, depression, post-traumatic symptoms and can also help increase emotional resilience. Psychological flexibility involves three components – mindfulness, emotional regulation, and commitment to values.

When we are psychologically flexible, we make decisions based on our chosen goals and values rather than our short-term emotional reactions.

4. IT TEACHES YOU TO BUILD AND MAINTAIN INTEROCEPTION

Interoception is a skill where we increase our internal awareness of our body by developing a felt sense of the body. When we have this new felt sense, we can logically connect our triggers to our body's responses. We can then apply somatic techniques to send safety signals from the body back up to the brain. When this process is repeated, we are essentially rewiring the brain and nervous system.

5. IT WAS ORIGINALLY CREATED BY A THERAPIST FOR PERSONAL USE.

As a therapist, I've helped people for years, providing insightful reflections, practical coping skills, and guided healing of deeply programed negative belief systems.

When I encountered anxiety and unwanted patterns in my own life, I realized I wasn't consistently offering myself the same compassion and reprogramming tools that I would provide to my clients.

I felt stuck in my own mental health journey. I knew journaling was a helpful tool, but I found it boring at times, and I couldn't keep a consistent habit. I tried many journaling methods, and they didn't feel right for me.

I started experimenting with creating my own journaling method, and that's how The Happy Brain Journal was born. I created this journal to help me stay consistent with habits that are essential for optimal mental health.

The best time to plant a tree was 20 years ago. The second-best time is now.

CHINESE PROVERB

How it works

Here we will walk through each part of the journal so you can feel confident about how each exercise works.

Daytime Routine

There are four exercises in the daytime routine. Below are brief descriptions of each exercise with examples. *It takes about 7 minutes to complete the daytime routine.*

1) Clear: This exercise is designed to help you do two things: face your fears and develop interoception. Fear, worry, and stress grow uncontrollably when we don't face them head on. We must name it to tame it! Interoception is a key component to taming your fears as it takes more than a logical awareness of a fear to overcome it. We must fully feel the uncomfortable sensations that are associated with fear to truly overcome it.

Interoception is an internal awareness of the body which is the foundation for learning psychological flexibility and rewiring the brain and nervous system.

2) RVRR Part I: Part one of the RVRR technique is designed to build new brain pathways for dealing with uncomfortable emotions and stressful situations. It does this through guiding you to build endurance for internal processing of the sensations that accompany stress and then teaching you how to effectively hold them in a healthy way so you can tend to your daily activities. This is psychological flexibility in action.

3) Picture: This exercise is designed to teach your brain to hold focused attention on one aspect of a desired outcome at a time. Learning to focus on one aspect at a time can increase your capacity for experiencing satisfaction throughout the journey while working on your goals.

This deliberate use of visualization will prime your brain to achieve goals and be open to opportunities.

4) Look: This exercise is designed to help you develop a strong sense of self, improve your self-esteem, and feel confident in your values. A strong sense of self is a key component to being able to maintain psychological flexibility.

Nighttime Routine

There are five exercises in the nighttime routine. Below are brief descriptions of each exercise with examples. *It takes about 7 minutes to complete the nighttime routine.*

1) List: This exercise is designed to teach your brain to scan for positive outcomes. The more practice your brain gets scanning for and identifying positive outcomes; the more your brain will begin to identify favorable or positive outcomes on its own. When done repeatedly, this exercise can override old programing and essentially rewire the brain. Once new brain pathways are formed this effect can then trickle down to the body, creating a sense of safety within your internal experience. When a person feels safe, they are more likely to take positive risks and perform better in several areas of life including work, sports, and relationships. This exercise calls for noticing "new" and "small things." This is especially effective when creating new neural pathways.

2) RVRR Part II: Part two of the RVRR technique is the final and essential piece in maintaining a healthy and happy environment in the brain and nervous system. Without part two of the RVRR technique, the emotions that are being initially processed and stored in part one of RVRR would overflow and create further distress. RVRR Part II is the actual physical instruction on how to fully process unwanted emotions out of the body.

This part of the journal exercise also helps keep you accountable to yourself. Keeping small promises to yourself helps build a foundation of security, stability, and trust within you. This foundation is the springboard from where healthy self-esteem and confidence can grow.

3) Visualize: This is a somatic exercise designed to help your body and nervous system experience relaxation. This exercise is also designed to train your nervous system to build endurance for staying in a relaxed state for an extended period. The more we practice creating a deliberate experience of relaxation in the body, the more the nervous system will be primed for experiencing the same in real life. Increasing your endurance for feeling this sensation can help heal an over exhausted nervous system and change the way you present yourself in the world.

4) Identify: This exercise is designed to teach your brain to scan for gratitude. There are a multitude of studies showing that gratitude can significantly improve mental health and overall happiness and satisfaction with life. This exercise is also designed to train your nervous system to become familiar with the sensations of gratitude and to build endurance for feeling gratitude for extended periods of time. Increasing your endurance for gratitude can help heal an over exhausted nervous system and improve stress tolerance. This exercise calls for noticing "new" and "small things." This is especially effective when creating new neural pathways.

5) Identify: This exercise is designed to help you get in touch with the messages stored on the subconscious level of the brain. Listening to your subconscious can help you make decisions that are more aligned with your true happiness and desires. Having a clear understanding of your true needs and desires can help increase your effectiveness and efficiency while reaching your goals. The use of third person in this exercise is deliberate and especially useful in this endeavor.

The Tools

Here you can find step by step instructions to learn how to do the RVRR Technique.

The RVRR Technique (pronounced "river")

The **RVRR** Technique stands for **R**egulate, **V**ault, **R**espond & **R**elease. This technique is divided into two parts. Part one includes (Regulate, Vault, Respond). Part two includes (Release). Below are instructions for how to do each part of the RVRR Technique:

RVRR Part I

Once mastered takes less than 60 seconds to complete

Regulate

1) Notice that you have an uncomfortable thought or situation and say it out loud in your mind. Label the emotion. *(example: "My boss asked me to come in for a meeting. I'm feeling anxiety")*

2) Use your imagination to scan your body and locate where you can sense the uncomfortable emotion. *(example: "I feel it in my chest")*

3) Describe the sensation that you feel in that body part. *(example: "It feels tight and heavy in my chest.")*

4) Take 5-20 seconds to feel the full strength and discomfort of these unwanted sensations. (As you practice you will build endurance to last longer)

5) Imagine a little ball of light floating in front of you *(with the most soothing color and voice)*. Imagine the little ball says to you *"I've got you"*

6) Take a deep breath and imagine the ball of light moving into your body and systematically toppling the uncomfortable emotions causing a chain reaction like falling dominoes. See and feel as the emotions fall in sequence.

Vault

1) Imagine a strong and secure vault floating in a corner of your environment *(choose whatever corner feels right for you)*.

2) Slowly breathe out and imagine the emotions leaving your body with your breath and into the vault.

3) Imagine closing the door and locking up all the unwanted emotions inside this ultra secure vault. Set a code on the vault for the time and day when you will come back to release the vault. The vault will sit patiently in your designated corner until it's time to revisit it.

4) Take another deep breath and imagine the little ball of light filling your body with strength and calm.

Respond

1) Now respond to your present situation based on your values and bigger picture goals.

RVRR Part II

Once mastered takes less than 5 minutes to complete

Release

1) Choose a physical movement that feels cathartic and is accessible to do. (for example: walking, stomping, jogging, jumping, punching a pillow or a punching bag, push-ups, scribbling in a journal, curling up into a ball and rocking back and forth, squeezing hands into tight fists, screaming into a pillow, crying, singing, growling, etc..)

2) Choose a color that you can associate with the emotions that are locked up in your vault.

3) Unlock your vault and allow the emotions to come back into your body where they were before. Think about the original situation that caused the uncomfortable emotions.

4) Use your imagination to envision these unwanted emotions inside your body with the color you have chosen.

5) Take 20-60 seconds to feel the full strength and discomfort of these unwanted sensations inside your body; Noticing where you feel them in your body. Stay with the uncomfortable sensations even if they move around to different body parts. Even if it gets stronger - stay in there as long as you can. (As you practice you will build endurance to last longer)

6) **Do** the physical movement you selected. Imagine the emotion together with the color leaving your body for good. Imagine this emotion/color being expressed out of your body and somewhere into your physical environment where it can be recycled and no longer bothers you.

Examples for RVRR Part II

A) As you sing you imagine red/anger leaving through your mouth and it's recycled into the sky.

B) As you walk you imagine orange/anxiety leaving through your feet and it's recycled into the earth.

C) As you punch a punching bag you imagine green/jealousy leaving through your hands and it's recycled into the punching bag.

D) As you do push-ups you imagine purple/frustration leaving your chest and it's recycled into the ground.

E) As you are curled up in a ball rocking back and forth you imagine blue/sadness leaving from your entire body where it's recycled into the air.

F) As you are crying you imagine yellow/shame leaving through your tears where it's recycled into the air as the tears evaporate.

G) As you are growling you imagine grey/anger leaving your throat and it's recycled into the mountains on the horizon.

H) As you bounce a basketball you imagine orange/frustration leaving from your chest, through your arms and hands into the ball where it exits onto the pavement.

G) As you squeeze your fists you imagine green/anxiety leaving from your throat through your arms, through your hands, through the air into the ground.

Write down your own ideas for releasing your vault:

1) _____

2) _____

3) _____

4) _____

5) _____

6) _____

7) _____

8) _____

9) _____

10) _____

Journal Entry Examples

Here you will see journal entry examples so you can feel confident about doing each exercise.

Starting My Day   01/11/2024

Clear out some mental space. Briefly describe the strongest thought or stressor that is on your mind – Label the emotion.

My boss sent an email last night saying he wants to have a meeting with me at the end of the week. I'm worried I'm going to be put on a performance improvement plan. I'm feeling anxiety.

Body Location: *Chest*   Body Sensation: *Pressure*

RVRR Part 1: Take a minute to perform part 1 of the RVRR technique. Now, set a plan for when, where and how you will release your vault later today. Write your plan below:

After work at 7pm tonight I can punch a punching bag at the gym.

Picture just one aspect of your ultimate dream life: Do not plan or strategize about how it's going to happen. **Just picture the final result**. Soften your gaze/or close your eyes and take a few deep breaths as you imagine and connect this part of your ultimate dream life. **Take a full minute** to **enjoy** this experience. How does this part of your ultimate dream life look and feel? Write the words "What if...?" and then describe this specific aspect of your ultimate dream life.

What if... I'm driving my new convertible on a scenic highway. As I feel the wind on my face, I also feel secure and strong knowing I have a leadership position in my company and my finances are overflowing with abundance.

Look deep into yourself: See and feel who you are at your core - your values, essence, innate abilities, and your heart. What images and qualities represent the real you? **Affirm** your unique personality. List the words that best describe you:

I am creative and resilient. I am trustworthy and hard working.

Ending My Day 01/11/2024

List two things that went your way today. [Even the smallest things are good to notice]

1. _My usual lunch spot had my favorite sandwich on the menu today._

2. _A friend sent me an encouraging text message today._

RVRR Part 2: Did you release your vault? How did it go? Write about it here:

I kept my word. I punched the punching bag after work and imagined red anxiety coming out of my fists.

Visualize a person, place, animal, or higher self that makes you feel safe and loved: **Imagine** and feel this essence. Soften your gaze/or close your eyes and take a few deep breaths as you connect. **Feel** and sense the loving, caring, and safe contact. Allow yourself to **melt** into the most soothing and comforting embrace. Allow yourself to **stay here for a full minute**. Is there a **sensation** or a **message** that comes to you? **Where** do you feel it in your body? List the words that best describe this experience:

I felt a warm comforting sensation on my face and chest. I'll be okay.

Identify one thing you are **grateful** for today: Make sure it's different from what you identified yesterday. [Even the smallest things count] Soften your gaze/or close your eyes and take a few deep breaths as you **take a full minute** to **savor** this feeling of gratitude. Write the details below:

I'm grateful for my dog who always greets me with a happy tail wag. I feel love and belonging.

Identify a current **need**. Go inside and ask yourself "what do I need?" Write in third person "your name needs":

Jake needs to feel important and wanted.

Starting My Day   01/12/2024

Clear out some mental space. Briefly describe the strongest thought or stressor that is on your mind – Label the emotion

<u>My partner is acting distant. I'm worried he is going to break up with me. I'm feeling fear and sadness.</u>

Body Location: <u>Stomach</u>   Body Sensation: <u>Sinking</u>

RVRR Part 1: Take a minute to perform part 1 of the RVRR technique. Now, set a plan for when, where and how you will release your vault later today. Write your plan below:

<u>When I get home from work, I can sing a song while crying.</u>

Picture just one aspect of your ultimate dream life: Do not plan or strategize about how it's going to happen. **Just picture the final result**. Soften your gaze/or close your eyes and take a few deep breaths as you imagine and connect this part of your ultimate dream life. **Take a full minute** to **enjoy** this experience. How does this part of your ultimate dream life look and feel? Write the words "What if...?" and then describe this specific aspect of your ultimate dream life.

<u>What if... I'm on a summer vacation in Italy with my fiancé. As we hold hands walking down the cobblestone streets, I feel excited and secure.</u>

Look deep into yourself: See and feel who you are at your core - your values, essence, innate abilities, and your heart. What images and qualities represent the real you? **Affirm** your unique personality. List the words that best describe you:

<u>I am loving, caring and fun. I'm smart and strong.</u>

Ending My Day   01/12/2024

List two things that went your way today. [Even the smallest things are good to notice]

1. <u>I got a good parking spot at work today.</u>

2. <u>A cute dog came up to me and let me pet him during my walk today.</u>

RVRR Part 2: Did you release your vault? How did it go? Write about it here:

<u>I kept my promise to myself. When I got home, I sang a song and cried while imagining the color grey coming through my tears.</u>

Visualize a person, place, animal, or higher self that makes you feel safe and loved: **Imagine** and feel this essence. Soften your gaze/or close your eyes and take a few deep breaths as you connect. **Feel** and sense the loving, caring, and safe contact. Allow yourself to **melt** into the most soothing and comforting embrace. Allow yourself to **stay here for a full minute**. Is there a **sensation** or a **message** that comes to you? **Where** do you feel it in your body? List the words that best describe this experience:

<u>I felt a soft yellow color giving me a gentle hug on my back and shoulders. I am lovable.</u>

Identify one thing you are **grateful** for today: Make sure it's different from what you identified yesterday. [Even the smallest things count] Soften your gaze/or close your eyes and take a few deep breaths as you **take a full minute** to **savor** this feeling of gratitude. Write the details below:

<u>I'm grateful for my co-worker who sends me funny memes throughout the day.</u>

Identify a current **need**. Go inside and ask yourself "what do I need?" Write in third person "your name needs":

<u>Morgan needs to feel desired and chosen.</u>

Starting My Day   01/13/2024

Clear out some mental space. Briefly describe the strongest thought or stressor that is on your mind – Label the emotion

<u>My in-laws are judging me about my life choices and my partner isn't standing up to them. I'm feeling frustrated.</u>

Body Location: <u>Arms and legs</u>   Body Sensation: <u>Hot and pressure</u>

RVRR Part 1: Take a minute to perform part 1 of the RVRR technique. Now, set a plan for when, where and how you will release your vault later today. Write your plan below:

<u>During my lunch break I can take a walk and imagine the frustration coming out of my body onto the pavement.</u>

Picture just one aspect of your ultimate dream life: Do not plan or strategize about how it's going to happen. **Just picture the final result**. Soften your gaze/or close your eyes and take a few deep breaths as you imagine and connect this part of your ultimate dream life. **Take a full minute** to **enjoy** this experience. How does this part of your ultimate dream life look and feel? Write the words "What if...?" and then describe this specific aspect of your ultimate dream life.

<u>What if... I'm in my new beach home that is perfectly decorated to my liking. I hear the ocean waves outside and I feel satisfied, relaxed and happy.</u>

Look deep into yourself: See and feel who you are at your core - your values, essence, innate abilities, and your heart. What images and qualities represent the real you? **Affirm** your unique personality. List the words that best describe you:

<u>I am creative and funny.</u>

Ending My Day   01/13/2024

List two things that went your way today. [Even the smallest things are good to notice]

1. <u>The sweater I wanted was available in my size and favorite color.</u>

2. <u>My neighbor smiled at me today at the entrance to my building.</u>

RVRR Part 2: Did you release your vault? How did it go? Write about it here:

<u>I did not keep my promise. I got distracted with work today and didn't get a chance to take a walk. I will set an alarm and try again tomorrow at 12pm.</u>

Visualize a person, place, animal, or higher self that makes you feel safe and loved: **Imagine** and feel this essence. Soften your gaze/or close your eyes and take a few deep breaths as you connect. **Feel** and sense the loving, caring, and safe contact. Allow yourself to **melt** into the most soothing and comforting embrace. Allow yourself to **stay here for a full minute**. Is there a **sensation** or a **message** that comes to you? **Where** do you feel it in your body? List the words that best describe this experience:

<u>I felt a soft purple with the smell of lavender soothing my stomach and back. I am safe.</u>

Identify one thing you are **grateful** for today: Make sure it's different from what you identified yesterday. [Even the smallest things count] Soften your gaze/or close your eyes and take a few deep breaths as you **take a full minute** to **savor** this feeling of gratitude. Write the details below:

<u>I'm grateful for my comfort TV shows that help me unwind.</u>

Identify a current **need**. Go inside and ask yourself "what do I need?" Write in third person "your name needs":

<u>Jillian needs to feel supported.</u>

FAQ

Here you can find answers to some of the most frequently asked questions.

Why is there such little space to write in the journal?

This journal is designed to be experiential. It's more about experiencing the exercises. Practicing them internally and then jotting down a few words to keep you accountable and remember what the experience was like.

How exactly does manifestation work and how does the Happy Brain Journal help increase my ability to manifest?

The "Many Worlds Interpretation" is a quantum mechanics theory created by physicist Hugh Everett in 1954 and has gained popularity by some modern-day theoretical physicists such as Sean Carroll.

The many worlds theory proposes that whenever an event occurs the universe splits into separate, parallel universes, each containing a different possible outcome. This creates a branching timeline where every potential reality exists simultaneously.

Some thought leaders who study the link between spirituality and quantum physics state we have the capacity to tap into these different timelines through frequency matching. Our frequency is determined by our thoughts, feelings and actions.

As we change our thoughts, feelings and actions we change our frequency to match the frequency of other parallel outcomes. When we are intentional about choosing which thoughts, feelings and actions we want to increase we are essentially choosing a new reality. You can think of it like changing radio stations. This is manifestation.

The Happy Brain Journal helps you manifest and reach your goals by teaching your brain to visualize your desired goal while training your nervous system to feel somatic safety and stay with these positive emotions for a longer period. It also teaches your brain to scan and look for positive outcomes that help maintain the felt sense of safety in your body for longer.

To manifest effectively, all three components must be aligned: Thoughts, feelings and actions. If you visualize your goal but feel scarcity and fear in your body and don't take consistent action steps you won't see any results.

The Happy Brain Journal also trains your brain to keep small promises to yourself when you check in daily about finishing part II of the RVRR Technique. As your brain develops a habit of keeping small promises to yourself, not only will you become more confident, but you will be more likely to keep other small promises to yourself such as small steps that help you reach your desired goals.

If I have negative thoughts or difficult emotions does that mean I won't manifest?

This is a common misconception. As humans we are meant to have a wide spectrum of thoughts and emotions as we experience the natural ups and downs of life. This is normal and healthy. Staying stuck for a prolonged period in a negative state can slow down your manifestations but having the normal ups and downs will not.

This is where the RVRR technique really shines. The RVRR technique teaches you to metabolize difficult emotions through your nervous system and out of your body. We don't want to have a buildup of negative emotions in our body as this can not only cause mental and physical illness but can also slow down our manifestations.

Believing that you must think positive thoughts and have positive emotions 24/7 is unrealistic and unhealthy.

A healthier, more realistic and efficient approach is to accept that negative thoughts and difficult emotions are a part of life, and we just need to use tools such as the RVRR technique to help process them out of our body. Sometimes it will be quick and sometimes it can take a longer time, depending on what type of life stressors are going on at the time.

If you are going through an extreme life stressor or dealing with a mental illness you cannot rely on the RVRR technique alone. In these cases, you need to seek treatment from a licensed medical professional and receive support from your community, family and friends to help stabilize your physical and mental health.

Will the RVRR Technique completely get rid of a difficult emotion every time?

The RVRR Technique is powerful and effective, however nothing in life is foolproof. Just like most things in life, it takes consistent practice to see the strongest and best results. The best way to use the RVRR technique is to practice daily with smaller emotions. This will build neural pathways for the RVRR Technique and as time goes on it will become more and more effective with bigger and bigger emotions.

Think of it like becoming a weightlifter. You can have the best tools and techniques, but you can't start with 200lbs on your first day. You must start with a light weight. Depending on your personal physiology maybe a light weight for you is 10lbs or 30lbs etc. You start small and gradually with consistent practice; you start to build up weight. Eventually you will be able to do the heavy lifting. The same principle goes for the RVRR Technique.

Sometimes you'll find that the RVVR Technique gives you complete relief of an uncomfortable emotion. Other times you'll find that it gives you partial relief and you'll need to repeat the technique again and then receive emotional support from a family member, friend or professional to get a little more relief. The more you practice over time the better results you'll have.

Why do I feel bored or anxious when I'm doing some of the exercises in this journal?

Many people have a low tolerance for feeling sensations of safety and calm in their body. This is because the nervous system feels the most comfortable with the "familiar." For many people, a constant state of stress and functional freeze are familiar sensations.

The nervous system can sometimes misinterpret sensations of safety and calm as boring or even dangerous. Think of it as the body's way of showing distrust of positive sensations and waiting for the other shoe to drop.

Through consistent and intentional exposure to sensations of safety and calm we can rewire our nervous system and allow space for more positive experiences to manifest into our lives.

The RVRR Technique has so many steps. Is it going to take a long time to do?

The RVRR technique is a highly effective somatic and experiential exercise that can build new brain pathways and bring healing to the nervous system. It has been broken down into many micro steps to help the reader understand how to perform the technique accurately.

Once you do the RVRR technique a few times you will start to get the hang of it and eventually master it just like riding a bike. If you were to break down how to ride a bike into micro steps it would feel daunting at first, but after a bit of practice you start to build a muscle memory for it and the entire experience just flows.

Think of it like learning to ride a bike. Soon you will just "know" how to do it without needing to read the steps. After you develop this inner knowing, it should take less than 60 seconds to perform part one and 2-5 minutes to complete part two of the RVRR technique.

If I only do the RVRR technique in this journal how is that going to help achieve psychological flexibility in the real world?

Once you start practicing the RVRR technique through this journal you'll start to build new neural pathways for it (like building muscle memory from practicing a sport). The goal is for this technique to become second nature and for you to start doing it in your real life - outside of this journal in real time, as you encounter challenging situations in your everyday life. Every time you successfully manage emotions and choose behaviors that are in line with your goals and values you get closer to building your dream life.

As you develop psychological flexibility, you'll find that life challenges won't weigh you down as much as they did before. You'll be able to metabolize negative emotions out of your nervous system much faster than before. The negative emotions will start to take more of a back seat, and you'll have an increased capacity for focusing on the positive and for feeling motivated about your life goals.

Excellence is not an act but a habit.

ARISTOTLE

***The* Happy Brain Journal:** The Most Powerful Way to Manifest, Feel Motivated and Improve Self-Esteem

Starting My Day _____/_____/_____

Clear out some mental space. *Briefly describe the strongest thought or stressor that is on your mind – Label the emotion.*

_____

_____

_____

Body Location: _____ Body Sensation: _____

RVRR Part 1: Take a minute to perform part 1 of the RVRR technique. Now, set a plan for when, where and how you will release your vault later today. *Write your plan below:*

_____

_____

_____

Picture just one aspect of your ultimate dream life: Do not plan or strategize about how it's going to happen. **Just picture the final result**. Soften your gaze/or close your eyes and take a few deep breaths as you imagine and connect this part of your ultimate dream life. **Take a full minute** to **enjoy** this experience. How does this part of your ultimate dream life look and feel? *Write the words "What if...?" and then describe this specific aspect of your ultimate dream life.*

_____

_____

_____

_____

_____

Look deep into yourself: See and feel who you are at your core - your values, essence, innate abilities, and your heart. What images and qualities represent the real you? **Affirm** your unique personality. *List the words that best describe you:*

_____

_____

_____

_____

_____

Ending My Day _____/_____/_____

List two things that went your way today. [Even the smallest things are good to notice]

1._____

2._____

RVRR Part 2: Did you release your vault? How did it go? *Write about it here:*
_____
_____

Visualize a person, place, animal, or higher self that makes you feel safe and loved: **Imagine** and feel this essence. Soften your gaze/or close your eyes and take a few deep breaths as you connect. **Feel** and sense the loving, caring, and safe contact. Allow yourself to **melt** into the most soothing and comforting embrace. Allow yourself to **stay here for a full minute**. Is there a **sensation** or a **message** that comes to you? **Where** do you feel it in your body? *List the words that best describe this experience:*
_____
_____
_____

Identify one thing you are **grateful** for today: Make sure it's different from what you identified yesterday. [Even the smallest things count] Soften your gaze/or close your eyes and take a few deep breaths as you **take a full minute** to **savor** this feeling of gratitude. *Write the details below:*
_____
_____

Identify a current **need**. Go inside and ask yourself "what do I need?" *Write in third person "your name needs":*
_____
_____

Starting My Day _____/_____/_____

Clear out some mental space. *Briefly describe the strongest thought or stressor that is on your mind – Label the emotion.*

_____

_____

_____

Body Location: _____ Body Sensation: _____

RVRR Part 1: Take a minute to perform part 1 of the RVRR technique. Now, set a plan for when, where and how you will release your vault later today. *Write your plan below:*

_____

_____

_____

Picture just one aspect of your ultimate dream life: Do not plan or strategize about how it's going to happen. **Just picture the final result.** Soften your gaze/or close your eyes and take a few deep breaths as you imagine and connect this part of your ultimate dream life. **Take a full minute** to **enjoy** this experience. How does this part of your ultimate dream life look and feel? *Write the words "What if…?" and then describe this specific aspect of your ultimate dream life.*

_____

_____

_____

_____

_____

Look deep into yourself: See and feel who you are at your core - your values, essence, innate abilities, and your heart. What images and qualities represent the real you? **Affirm** your unique personality. *List the words that best describe you:*

_____

_____

_____

_____

Ending My Day _____/_____/_____

List two things that went your way today. [Even the smallest things are good to notice]

1._____

2._____

RVRR Part 2: Did you release your vault? How did it go? *Write about it here:*
_____
_____
_____

Visualize a person, place, animal, or higher self that makes you feel safe and loved: **Imagine** and feel this essence. Soften your gaze/or close your eyes and take a few deep breaths as you connect. **Feel** and sense the loving, caring, and safe contact. Allow yourself to **melt** into the most soothing and comforting embrace. Allow yourself to **stay here for a full minute**. Is there a **sensation** or a **message** that comes to you? **Where** do you feel it in your body? *List the words that best describe this experience:*
_____
_____
_____

Identify one thing you are **grateful** for today: Make sure it's different from what you identified yesterday. [Even the smallest things count] Soften your gaze/or close your eyes and take a few deep breaths as you **take a full minute** to **savor** this feeling of gratitude. *Write the details below:*
_____
_____
_____

Identify a current **need**. Go inside and ask yourself "what do I need?" *Write in third person "your name needs":*
_____
_____
_____

Starting My Day _____/_____/_____

Clear out some mental space. *Briefly describe the strongest thought or stressor that is on your mind – Label the emotion.*

_____

_____

_____

Body Location: _____ Body Sensation: _____

RVRR Part 1: Take a minute to perform part 1 of the RVRR technique. Now, set a plan for when, where and how you will release your vault later today. *Write your plan below:*

_____

_____

_____

Picture just one aspect of your ultimate dream life: Do not plan or strategize about how it's going to happen. **Just picture the final result.** Soften your gaze/or close your eyes and take a few deep breaths as you imagine and connect this part of your ultimate dream life. **Take a full minute** to **enjoy** this experience. How does this part of your ultimate dream life look and feel? *Write the words "What if…?" and then describe this specific aspect of your ultimate dream life.*

_____

_____

_____

_____

_____

Look deep into yourself: See and feel who you are at your core - your values, essence, innate abilities, and your heart. What images and qualities represent the real you? **Affirm** your unique personality. *List the words that best describe you:*

_____

_____

_____

_____

Ending My Day _____ / _____ / _____

List two things that went your way today. [Even the smallest things are good to notice]

1._____
2._____

RVRR Part 2: Did you release your vault? How did it go? *Write about it here:*
_____
_____
_____

Visualize a person, place, animal, or higher self that makes you feel safe and loved: **Imagine** and feel this essence. Soften your gaze/or close your eyes and take a few deep breaths as you connect. **Feel** and sense the loving, caring, and safe contact. Allow yourself to **melt** into the most soothing and comforting embrace. Allow yourself to **stay here for a full minute.** Is there a **sensation** or a **message** that comes to you? **Where** do you feel it in your body? *List the words that best describe this experience:*
_____
_____
_____
_____

Identify one thing you are **grateful** for today: Make sure it's different from what you identified yesterday. [Even the smallest things count] Soften your gaze/or close your eyes and take a few deep breaths as you **take a full minute** to **savor** this feeling of gratitude. *Write the details below:*
_____
_____
_____

Identify a current **need**. Go inside and ask yourself "what do I need?" *Write in third person "your name needs":*
_____
_____
_____

Starting My Day _____/_____/_____

Clear out some mental space. *Briefly describe the strongest thought or stressor that is on your mind – Label the emotion.*

_____

_____

_____

Body Location: _____ Body Sensation: _____

RVRR Part 1: Take a minute to perform part 1 of the RVRR technique. Now, set a plan for when, where and how you will release your vault later today. *Write your plan below:*

_____

_____

_____

Picture just one aspect of your ultimate dream life: Do not plan or strategize about how it's going to happen. **Just picture the final result**. Soften your gaze/or close your eyes and take a few deep breaths as you imagine and connect this part of your ultimate dream life. **Take a full minute** to **enjoy** this experience. How does this part of your ultimate dream life look and feel? *Write the words "What if...?" and then describe this specific aspect of your ultimate dream life.*

_____

_____

_____

_____

_____

Look deep into yourself: See and feel who you are at your core - your values, essence, innate abilities, and your heart. What images and qualities represent the real you? **Affirm** your unique personality. *List the words that best describe you:*

_____

_____

_____

_____

Ending My Day _____/_____/_____

List two things that went your way today. [Even the smallest things are good to notice]

1._____

2._____

RVRR Part 2: Did you release your vault? How did it go? *Write about it here:*

_____

_____

Visualize a person, place, animal, or higher self that makes you feel safe and loved: **Imagine** and feel this essence. Soften your gaze/or close your eyes and take a few deep breaths as you connect. **Feel** and sense the loving, caring, and safe contact. Allow yourself to **melt** into the most soothing and comforting embrace. Allow yourself to **stay here for a full minute**. Is there a **sensation** or a **message** that comes to you? **Where** do you feel it in your body? *List the words that best describe this experience:*

_____

_____

_____

Identify one thing you are **grateful** for today: Make sure it's different from what you identified yesterday. [Even the smallest things count] Soften your gaze/or close your eyes and take a few deep breaths as you **take a full minute** to **savor** this feeling of gratitude. *Write the details below:*

_____

_____

Identify a current **need**. Go inside and ask yourself "what do I need?" *Write in third person "your name needs":*

_____

_____

Starting My Day _____/_____/_____

Clear out some mental space. *Briefly describe the strongest thought or stressor that is on your mind – Label the emotion.*

_____

_____

_____

Body Location: _____ Body Sensation: _____

RVRR Part 1: Take a minute to perform part 1 of the RVRR technique. Now, set a plan for when, where and how you will release your vault later today. *Write your plan below:*

_____

_____

_____

Picture just one aspect of your ultimate dream life: Do not plan or strategize about how it's going to happen. **Just picture the final result.** Soften your gaze/or close your eyes and take a few deep breaths as you imagine and connect this part of your ultimate dream life. **Take a full minute** to **enjoy** this experience. How does this part of your ultimate dream life look and feel? *Write the words "What if…?" and then describe this specific aspect of your ultimate dream life.*

_____

_____

_____

_____

_____

Look deep into yourself: See and feel who you are at your core - your values, essence, innate abilities, and your heart. What images and qualities represent the real you? **Affirm** your unique personality. *List the words that best describe you:*

_____

_____

_____

_____

Ending My Day _____/_____/_____

List two things that went your way today. [Even the smallest things are good to notice]

1._____

2._____

RVRR Part 2: Did you release your vault? How did it go? *Write about it here:*

_____

_____

Visualize a person, place, animal, or higher self that makes you feel safe and loved: **Imagine** and feel this essence. Soften your gaze/or close your eyes and take a few deep breaths as you connect. **Feel** and sense the loving, caring, and safe contact. Allow yourself to **melt** into the most soothing and comforting embrace. Allow yourself to **stay here for a full minute**. Is there a **sensation** or a **message** that comes to you? **Where** do you feel it in your body? *List the words that best describe this experience:*

_____

_____

_____

Identify one thing you are **grateful** for today: Make sure it's different from what you identified yesterday. [Even the smallest things count] Soften your gaze/or close your eyes and take a few deep breaths as you **take a full minute** to **savor** this feeling of gratitude. *Write the details below:*

_____

_____

Identify a current **need**. Go inside and ask yourself "what do I need?" *Write in third person "your name needs":*

_____

_____

Starting My Day _____/_____/_____

Clear out some mental space. *Briefly describe the strongest thought or stressor that is on your mind – Label the emotion.*

_____

_____

_____

Body Location: _____ Body Sensation: _____

RVRR Part 1: Take a minute to perform part 1 of the RVRR technique. Now, set a plan for when, where and how you will release your vault later today. *Write your plan below:*

_____

_____

_____

Picture just one aspect of your ultimate dream life: Do not plan or strategize about how it's going to happen. **Just picture the final result.** Soften your gaze/or close your eyes and take a few deep breaths as you imagine and connect this part of your ultimate dream life. **Take a full minute** to **enjoy** this experience. How does this part of your ultimate dream life look and feel? *Write the words "What if...?" and then describe this specific aspect of your ultimate dream life.*

_____

_____

_____

_____

_____

Look deep into yourself: See and feel who you are at your core - your values, essence, innate abilities, and your heart. What images and qualities represent the real you? **Affirm** your unique personality. *List the words that best describe you:*

_____

_____

_____

_____

_____

Ending My Day _____/_____/_____

List two things that went your way today. [Even the smallest things are good to notice]

1._____

2._____

RVRR Part 2: Did you release your vault? How did it go? *Write about it here:*
_____
_____
_____

Visualize a person, place, animal, or higher self that makes you feel safe and loved: **Imagine** and feel this essence. Soften your gaze/or close your eyes and take a few deep breaths as you connect. **Feel** and sense the loving, caring, and safe contact. Allow yourself to **melt** into the most soothing and comforting embrace. Allow yourself to **stay here for a full minute**. Is there a **sensation** or a **message** that comes to you? **Where** do you feel it in your body? *List the words that best describe this experience:*
_____
_____
_____
_____

Identify one thing you are **grateful** for today: Make sure it's different from what you identified yesterday. [Even the smallest things count] Soften your gaze/or close your eyes and take a few deep breaths as you **take a full minute** to **savor** this feeling of gratitude. *Write the details below:*
_____
_____
_____

Identify a current **need**. Go inside and ask yourself "what do I need?" *Write in third person "your name needs":*
_____
_____
_____

Starting My Day _____/_____/_____

Clear out some mental space. *Briefly describe the strongest thought or stressor that is on your mind – Label the emotion.*

_____

_____

_____

Body Location: _____ Body Sensation: _____

RVRR Part 1: Take a minute to perform part 1 of the RVRR technique. Now, set a plan for when, where and how you will release your vault later today. *Write your plan below:*

_____

_____

_____

Picture just one aspect of your ultimate dream life: Do not plan or strategize about how it's going to happen. **Just picture the final result**. Soften your gaze/or close your eyes and take a few deep breaths as you imagine and connect this part of your ultimate dream life. **Take a full minute** to **enjoy** this experience. How does this part of your ultimate dream life look and feel? *Write the words "What if...?" and then describe this specific aspect of your ultimate dream life.*

_____

_____

_____

_____

_____

Look deep into yourself: See and feel who you are at your core - your values, essence, innate abilities, and your heart. What images and qualities represent the real you? **Affirm** your unique personality. *List the words that best describe you:*

_____

_____

_____

_____

Ending My Day _____/_____/_____

List two things that went your way today. [Even the smallest things are good to notice]

1._____

2._____

RVRR Part 2: Did you release your vault? How did it go? *Write about it here:*

_____

_____

_____

Visualize a person, place, animal, or higher self that makes you feel safe and loved: **Imagine** and feel this essence. Soften your gaze/or close your eyes and take a few deep breaths as you connect. **Feel** and sense the loving, caring, and safe contact. Allow yourself to **melt** into the most soothing and comforting embrace. Allow yourself to **stay here for a full minute**. Is there a **sensation** or a **message** that comes to you? **Where** do you feel it in your body? *List the words that best describe this experience:*

_____

_____

_____

_____

Identify one thing you are **grateful** for today: Make sure it's different from what you identified yesterday. [Even the smallest things count] Soften your gaze/or close your eyes and take a few deep breaths as you **take a full minute** to **savor** this feeling of gratitude. *Write the details below:*

_____

_____

_____

Identify a current **need**. Go inside and ask yourself "what do I need?" *Write in third person "your name needs":*

_____

_____

_____

Starting My Day _____/_____/_____

Clear out some mental space. *Briefly describe the strongest thought or stressor that is on your mind – Label the emotion.*

_____

_____

_____

Body Location: _____ Body Sensation: _____

RVRR Part 1: Take a minute to perform part 1 of the RVRR technique. Now, set a plan for when, where and how you will release your vault later today. *Write your plan below:*

_____

_____

_____

Picture just one aspect of your ultimate dream life: Do not plan or strategize about how it's going to happen. **Just picture the final result.** Soften your gaze/or close your eyes and take a few deep breaths as you imagine and connect this part of your ultimate dream life. **Take a full minute** to **enjoy** this experience. How does this part of your ultimate dream life look and feel? *Write the words "What if...?" and then describe this specific aspect of your ultimate dream life.*

_____

_____

_____

_____

_____

Look deep into yourself: See and feel who you are at your core - your values, essence, innate abilities, and your heart. What images and qualities represent the real you? **Affirm** your unique personality. *List the words that best describe you:*

_____

_____

_____

_____

@QuantumMindframe

Ending My Day _____/_____/_____

List two things that went your way today. [Even the smallest things are good to notice]

1._____

2._____

RVRR Part 2: Did you release your vault? How did it go? *Write about it here:*

_____

_____

Visualize a person, place, animal, or higher self that makes you feel safe and loved: **Imagine** and feel this essence. Soften your gaze/or close your eyes and take a few deep breaths as you connect. **Feel** and sense the loving, caring, and safe contact. Allow yourself to **melt** into the most soothing and comforting embrace. Allow yourself to **stay here for a full minute.** Is there a **sensation** or a **message** that comes to you? **Where** do you feel it in your body? *List the words that best describe this experience:*

_____

_____

_____

Identify one thing you are **grateful** for today: Make sure it's different from what you identified yesterday. [Even the smallest things count] Soften your gaze/or close your eyes and take a few deep breaths as you **take a full minute** to **savor** this feeling of gratitude. *Write the details below:*

_____

_____

Identify a current **need**. Go inside and ask yourself "what do I need?" *Write in third person "your name needs":*

_____

_____

Starting My Day _____/_____/_____

Clear out some mental space. *Briefly describe the strongest thought or stressor that is on your mind – Label the emotion.*

_____
_____
_____

Body Location: _____ Body Sensation: _____

RVRR Part 1: Take a minute to perform part 1 of the RVRR technique. Now, set a plan for when, where and how you will release your vault later today. *Write your plan below:*

_____
_____
_____

Picture just one aspect of your ultimate dream life: Do not plan or strategize about how it's going to happen. **Just picture the final result.** Soften your gaze/or close your eyes and take a few deep breaths as you imagine and connect this part of your ultimate dream life. **Take a full minute** to **enjoy** this experience. How does this part of your ultimate dream life look and feel? *Write the words "What if…?" and then describe this specific aspect of your ultimate dream life.*

_____
_____
_____
_____
_____

Look deep into yourself: See and feel who you are at your core - your values, essence, innate abilities, and your heart. What images and qualities represent the real you? **Affirm** your unique personality. *List the words that best describe you:*

_____
_____
_____
_____

Ending My Day _____/_____/_____

List two things that went your way today. [Even the smallest things are good to notice]

1._____

2._____

RVRR Part 2: Did you release your vault? How did it go? *Write about it here:*
_____
_____
_____

Visualize a person, place, animal, or higher self that makes you feel safe and loved: **Imagine** and feel this essence. Soften your gaze/or close your eyes and take a few deep breaths as you connect. **Feel** and sense the loving, caring, and safe contact. Allow yourself to **melt** into the most soothing and comforting embrace. Allow yourself to **stay here for a full minute**. Is there a **sensation** or a **message** that comes to you? **Where** do you feel it in your body? *List the words that best describe this experience:*
_____
_____
_____
_____

Identify one thing you are **grateful** for today: Make sure it's different from what you identified yesterday. [Even the smallest things count] Soften your gaze/or close your eyes and take a few deep breaths as you **take a full minute** to **savor** this feeling of gratitude. *Write the details below:*
_____
_____
_____

Identify a current **need**. Go inside and ask yourself "what do I need?" *Write in third person "your name needs":*
_____
_____
_____

Starting My Day _____/_____/_____

Clear out some mental space. *Briefly describe the strongest thought or stressor that is on your mind – Label the emotion.*

_____

Body Location: _____ Body Sensation: _____

RVRR Part 1: Take a minute to perform part 1 of the RVRR technique. Now, set a plan for when, where and how you will release your vault later today. *Write your plan below:*

_____

Picture just one aspect of your ultimate dream life: Do not plan or strategize about how it's going to happen. **Just picture the final result**. Soften your gaze/or close your eyes and take a few deep breaths as you imagine and connect this part of your ultimate dream life. **Take a full minute** to **enjoy** this experience. How does this part of your ultimate dream life look and feel? *Write the words "What if…?" and then describe this specific aspect of your ultimate dream life.*

_____

Look deep into yourself: See and feel who you are at your core - your values, essence, innate abilities, and your heart. What images and qualities represent the real you? **Affirm** your unique personality. *List the words that best describe you:*

_____

Ending My Day _____/_____/_____

List two things that went your way today. [Even the smallest things are good to notice]

1._____

2._____

RVRR Part 2: Did you release your vault? How did it go? *Write about it here:*
_____
_____

Visualize a person, place, animal, or higher self that makes you feel safe and loved: **Imagine** and feel this essence. Soften your gaze/or close your eyes and take a few deep breaths as you connect. **Feel** and sense the loving, caring, and safe contact. Allow yourself to **melt** into the most soothing and comforting embrace. Allow yourself to **stay here for a full minute**. Is there a **sensation** or a **message** that comes to you? **Where** do you feel it in your body? *List the words that best describe this experience:*
_____
_____
_____

Identify one thing you are **grateful** for today: Make sure it's different from what you identified yesterday. [Even the smallest things count] Soften your gaze/or close your eyes and take a few deep breaths as you **take a full minute** to **savor** this feeling of gratitude. *Write the details below:*
_____
_____
_____

Identify a current **need**. Go inside and ask yourself "what do I need?" *Write in third person "your name needs":*
_____
_____

Starting My Day _____/_____/_____

Clear out some mental space. *Briefly describe the strongest thought or stressor that is on your mind – Label the emotion.*

_____

_____

_____

Body Location: _____ Body Sensation: _____

RVRR Part 1: Take a minute to perform part 1 of the RVRR technique. Now, set a plan for when, where and how you will release your vault later today. *Write your plan below:*

_____

_____

_____

Picture just one aspect of your ultimate dream life: Do not plan or strategize about how it's going to happen. **Just picture the final result.** Soften your gaze/or close your eyes and take a few deep breaths as you imagine and connect this part of your ultimate dream life. **Take a full minute** to **enjoy** this experience. How does this part of your ultimate dream life look and feel? *Write the words "What if...?" and then describe this specific aspect of your ultimate dream life.*

_____

_____

_____

_____

_____

Look deep into yourself: See and feel who you are at your core - your values, essence, innate abilities, and your heart. What images and qualities represent the real you? **Affirm** your unique personality. *List the words that best describe you:*

_____

_____

_____

_____

_____

@QuantumMindframe

Ending My Day _____/_____/_____

List two things that went your way today. [Even the smallest things are good to notice]

1._____

2._____

RVRR Part 2: Did you release your vault? How did it go? *Write about it here:*

_____
_____
_____

Visualize a person, place, animal, or higher self that makes you feel safe and loved: **Imagine** and feel this essence. Soften your gaze/or close your eyes and take a few deep breaths as you connect. **Feel** and sense the loving, caring, and safe contact. Allow yourself to **melt** into the most soothing and comforting embrace. Allow yourself to **stay here for a full minute**. Is there a **sensation** or a **message** that comes to you? **Where** do you feel it in your body? *List the words that best describe this experience:*

_____
_____
_____
_____

Identify one thing you are **grateful** for today: Make sure it's different from what you identified yesterday. [Even the smallest things count] Soften your gaze/or close your eyes and take a few deep breaths as you **take a full minute** to **savor** this feeling of gratitude. *Write the details below:*

_____
_____
_____

Identify a current **need**. Go inside and ask yourself "what do I need?" *Write in third person "your name needs":*

_____
_____
_____

Starting My Day _____/_____/_____

Clear out some mental space. *Briefly describe the strongest thought or stressor that is on your mind – Label the emotion.*

_____

_____

_____

Body Location: _____ Body Sensation: _____

RVRR Part 1: Take a minute to perform part 1 of the RVRR technique. Now, set a plan for when, where and how you will release your vault later today. *Write your plan below:*

_____

_____

_____

Picture just one aspect of your ultimate dream life: Do not plan or strategize about how it's going to happen. **Just picture the final result.** Soften your gaze/or close your eyes and take a few deep breaths as you imagine and connect this part of your ultimate dream life. **Take a full minute** to **enjoy** this experience. How does this part of your ultimate dream life look and feel? *Write the words "What if…?" and then describe this specific aspect of your ultimate dream life.*

_____

_____

_____

_____

_____

Look deep into yourself: See and feel who you are at your core - your values, essence, innate abilities, and your heart. What images and qualities represent the real you? **Affirm** your unique personality. *List the words that best describe you:*

_____

_____

_____

_____

@QuantumMindframe

Ending My Day _____/_____/_____

List two things that went your way today. [Even the smallest things are good to notice]

1._____

2._____

RVRR Part 2: Did you release your vault? How did it go? *Write about it here:*

_____
_____

Visualize a person, place, animal, or higher self that makes you feel safe and loved: **Imagine** and feel this essence. Soften your gaze/or close your eyes and take a few deep breaths as you connect. **Feel** and sense the loving, caring, and safe contact. Allow yourself to **melt** into the most soothing and comforting embrace. Allow yourself to **stay here for a full minute**. Is there a **sensation** or a **message** that comes to you? **Where** do you feel it in your body? *List the words that best describe this experience:*

_____
_____
_____

Identify one thing you are **grateful** for today: Make sure it's different from what you identified yesterday. [Even the smallest things count] Soften your gaze/or close your eyes and take a few deep breaths as you **take a full minute** to **savor** this feeling of gratitude. *Write the details below:*

_____
_____

Identify a current **need**. Go inside and ask yourself "what do I need?" *Write in third person "your name needs":*

_____
_____

Starting My Day _____/_____/_____

Clear out some mental space. *Briefly describe the strongest thought or stressor that is on your mind – Label the emotion.*

_____

_____

_____

Body Location: _____ Body Sensation: _____

RVRR Part 1: Take a minute to perform part 1 of the RVRR technique. Now, set a plan for when, where and how you will release your vault later today. *Write your plan below:*

_____

_____

_____

Picture just one aspect of your ultimate dream life: Do not plan or strategize about how it's going to happen. **Just picture the final result.** Soften your gaze/or close your eyes and take a few deep breaths as you imagine and connect this part of your ultimate dream life. **Take a full minute** to **enjoy** this experience. How does this part of your ultimate dream life look and feel? *Write the words "What if...?" and then describe this specific aspect of your ultimate dream life.*

_____

_____

_____

_____

_____

Look deep into yourself: See and feel who you are at your core - your values, essence, innate abilities, and your heart. What images and qualities represent the real you? **Affirm** your unique personality. *List the words that best describe you:*

_____

_____

_____

_____

Ending My Day _____/_____/_____

List two things that went your way today. [Even the smallest things are good to notice]

1. _____

2. _____

RVRR Part 2: Did you release your vault? How did it go? *Write about it here:*

_____
_____
_____

Visualize a person, place, animal, or higher self that makes you feel safe and loved: **Imagine** and feel this essence. Soften your gaze/or close your eyes and take a few deep breaths as you connect. **Feel** and sense the loving, caring, and safe contact. Allow yourself to **melt** into the most soothing and comforting embrace. Allow yourself to **stay here for a full minute**. Is there a **sensation** or a **message** that comes to you? **Where** do you feel it in your body? *List the words that best describe this experience:*

_____
_____
_____

Identify one thing you are **grateful** for today: Make sure it's different from what you identified yesterday. [Even the smallest things count] Soften your gaze/or close your eyes and take a few deep breaths as you **take a full minute** to **savor** this feeling of gratitude. *Write the details below:*

_____
_____
_____

Identify a current **need**. Go inside and ask yourself "what do I need?" *Write in third person "your name needs":*

_____
_____
_____

Starting My Day _____/_____/_____

Clear out some mental space. *Briefly describe the strongest thought or stressor that is on your mind – Label the emotion.*

_____

_____

_____

Body Location: _____ Body Sensation: _____

RVRR Part 1: Take a minute to perform part 1 of the RVRR technique. Now, set a plan for when, where and how you will release your vault later today. *Write your plan below:*

_____

_____

_____

Picture just one aspect of your ultimate dream life: Do not plan or strategize about how it's going to happen. **Just picture the final result.** Soften your gaze/or close your eyes and take a few deep breaths as you imagine and connect this part of your ultimate dream life. **Take a full minute** to **enjoy** this experience. How does this part of your ultimate dream life look and feel? *Write the words "What if...?" and then describe this specific aspect of your ultimate dream life.*

_____

_____

_____

_____

_____

Look deep into yourself: See and feel who you are at your core - your values, essence, innate abilities, and your heart. What images and qualities represent the real you? **Affirm** your unique personality. *List the words that best describe you:*

_____

_____

_____

_____

@QuantumMindframe

Ending My Day _____/_____/_____

List two things that went your way today. [Even the smallest things are good to notice]

1._____
2._____

RVRR Part 2: Did you release your vault? How did it go? *Write about it here:*
_____
_____
_____

Visualize a person, place, animal, or higher self that makes you feel safe and loved: **Imagine** and feel this essence. Soften your gaze/or close your eyes and take a few deep breaths as you connect. **Feel** and sense the loving, caring, and safe contact. Allow yourself to **melt** into the most soothing and comforting embrace. Allow yourself to **stay here for a full minute.** Is there a **sensation** or a **message** that comes to you? **Where** do you feel it in your body? *List the words that best describe this experience:*
_____
_____
_____
_____

Identify one thing you are **grateful** for today: Make sure it's different from what you identified yesterday. [Even the smallest things count] Soften your gaze/or close your eyes and take a few deep breaths as you **take a full minute** to **savor** this feeling of gratitude. *Write the details below:*
_____
_____
_____

Identify a current **need**. Go inside and ask yourself "what do I need?" *Write in third person "your name needs":*
_____
_____
_____

Starting My Day _____/_____/_____

Clear out some mental space. *Briefly describe the strongest thought or stressor that is on your mind – Label the emotion.*

_____

_____

_____

Body Location: _____ Body Sensation: _____

RVRR Part 1: Take a minute to perform part 1 of the RVRR technique. Now, set a plan for when, where and how you will release your vault later today. *Write your plan below:*

_____

_____

_____

Picture just one aspect of your ultimate dream life: Do not plan or strategize about how it's going to happen. **Just picture the final result.** Soften your gaze/or close your eyes and take a few deep breaths as you imagine and connect this part of your ultimate dream life. **Take a full minute** to **enjoy** this experience. How does this part of your ultimate dream life look and feel? *Write the words "What if…?" and then describe this specific aspect of your ultimate dream life.*

_____

_____

_____

_____

_____

_____

Look deep into yourself: See and feel who you are at your core - your values, essence, innate abilities, and your heart. What images and qualities represent the real you? **Affirm** your unique personality. *List the words that best describe you:*

_____

_____

_____

_____

Ending My Day _____/_____/_____

List two things that went your way today. [Even the smallest things are good to notice]

1._____

2._____

RVRR Part 2: Did you release your vault? How did it go? *Write about it here:*
_____
_____
_____

Visualize a person, place, animal, or higher self that makes you feel safe and loved: **Imagine** and feel this essence. Soften your gaze/or close your eyes and take a few deep breaths as you connect. **Feel** and sense the loving, caring, and safe contact. Allow yourself to **melt** into the most soothing and comforting embrace. Allow yourself to **stay here for a full minute.** Is there a **sensation** or a **message** that comes to you? **Where** do you feel it in your body? *List the words that best describe this experience:*
_____
_____
_____

Identify one thing you are **grateful** for today: Make sure it's different from what you identified yesterday. [Even the smallest things count] Soften your gaze/or close your eyes and take a few deep breaths as you **take a full minute** to **savor** this feeling of gratitude. *Write the details below:*
_____
_____

Identify a current **need**. Go inside and ask yourself "what do I need?" *Write in third person "your name needs":*
_____
_____

Starting My Day _____/_____/_____

Clear out some mental space. *Briefly describe the strongest thought or stressor that is on your mind – Label the emotion.*

_____
_____
_____

Body Location: _____ Body Sensation: _____

RVRR Part 1: Take a minute to perform part 1 of the RVRR technique. Now, set a plan for when, where and how you will release your vault later today. *Write your plan below:*

_____
_____
_____

Picture just one aspect of your ultimate dream life: Do not plan or strategize about how it's going to happen. **Just picture the final result.** Soften your gaze/or close your eyes and take a few deep breaths as you imagine and connect this part of your ultimate dream life. **Take a full minute** to **enjoy** this experience. How does this part of your ultimate dream life look and feel? *Write the words "What if...?" and then describe this specific aspect of your ultimate dream life.*

_____
_____
_____
_____
_____

Look deep into yourself: See and feel who you are at your core - your values, essence, innate abilities, and your heart. What images and qualities represent the real you? **Affirm** your unique personality. *List the words that best describe you:*

_____
_____
_____
_____

Ending My Day _____/_____/_____

List two things that went your way today. [Even the smallest things are good to notice]

1._____

2._____

RVRR Part 2: Did you release your vault? How did it go? *Write about it here:*

_____

_____

_____

Visualize a person, place, animal, or higher self that makes you feel safe and loved: **Imagine** and feel this essence. Soften your gaze/or close your eyes and take a few deep breaths as you connect. **Feel** and sense the loving, caring, and safe contact. Allow yourself to **melt** into the most soothing and comforting embrace. Allow yourself to **stay here for a full minute**. Is there a **sensation** or a **message** that comes to you? **Where** do you feel it in your body? *List the words that best describe this experience:*

_____

_____

_____

_____

Identify one thing you are **grateful** for today: Make sure it's different from what you identified yesterday. [Even the smallest things count] Soften your gaze/or close your eyes and take a few deep breaths as you **take a full minute** to **savor** this feeling of gratitude. *Write the details below:*

_____

_____

_____

Identify a current **need**. Go inside and ask yourself "what do I need?" *Write in third person "your name needs":*

_____

_____

_____

Starting My Day _____/_____/_____

Clear out some mental space. *Briefly describe the strongest thought or stressor that is on your mind – Label the emotion.*

_____

_____

_____

Body Location: _____ Body Sensation: _____

RVRR Part 1: Take a minute to perform part 1 of the RVRR technique. Now, set a plan for when, where and how you will release your vault later today. *Write your plan below:*

_____

_____

_____

Picture just one aspect of your ultimate dream life: Do not plan or strategize about how it's going to happen. **Just picture the final result.** Soften your gaze/or close your eyes and take a few deep breaths as you imagine and connect this part of your ultimate dream life. **Take a full minute** to **enjoy** this experience. How does this part of your ultimate dream life look and feel? *Write the words "What if...?" and then describe this specific aspect of your ultimate dream life.*

_____

_____

_____

_____

_____

Look deep into yourself: See and feel who you are at your core - your values, essence, innate abilities, and your heart. What images and qualities represent the real you? **Affirm** your unique personality. *List the words that best describe you:*

_____

_____

_____

_____

Ending My Day _____/_____/_____

List two things that went your way today. [Even the smallest things are good to notice]

1._____

2._____

RVRR Part 2: Did you release your vault? How did it go? *Write about it here:*

_____
_____
_____

Visualize a person, place, animal, or higher self that makes you feel safe and loved: **Imagine** and feel this essence. Soften your gaze/or close your eyes and take a few deep breaths as you connect. **Feel** and sense the loving, caring, and safe contact. Allow yourself to **melt** into the most soothing and comforting embrace. Allow yourself to **stay here for a full minute**. Is there a **sensation** or a **message** that comes to you? **Where** do you feel it in your body? *List the words that best describe this experience:*

_____
_____
_____
_____

Identify one thing you are **grateful** for today: Make sure it's different from what you identified yesterday. [Even the smallest things count] Soften your gaze/or close your eyes and take a few deep breaths as you **take a full minute** to **savor** this feeling of gratitude. *Write the details below:*

_____
_____
_____

Identify a current **need**. Go inside and ask yourself "what do I need?" *Write in third person "your name needs":*

_____
_____

Starting My Day _____/_____/_____

Clear out some mental space. *Briefly describe the strongest thought or stressor that is on your mind – Label the emotion.*

_____
_____
_____

Body Location: _____ Body Sensation: _____

RVRR Part 1: Take a minute to perform part 1 of the RVRR technique. Now, set a plan for when, where and how you will release your vault later today. *Write your plan below:*

_____
_____
_____

Picture just one aspect of your ultimate dream life: Do not plan or strategize about how it's going to happen. **Just picture the final result.** Soften your gaze/or close your eyes and take a few deep breaths as you imagine and connect this part of your ultimate dream life. **Take a full minute** to **enjoy** this experience. How does this part of your ultimate dream life look and feel? *Write the words "What if...?" and then describe this specific aspect of your ultimate dream life.*

_____
_____
_____
_____
_____

Look deep into yourself: See and feel who you are at your core - your values, essence, innate abilities, and your heart. What images and qualities represent the real you? **Affirm** your unique personality. *List the words that best describe you:*

_____
_____
_____
_____

Ending My Day _____/_____/_____

List two things that went your way today. [Even the smallest things are good to notice]

1._____

2._____

RVRR Part 2: Did you release your vault? How did it go? *Write about it here:*

_____

_____

_____

Visualize a person, place, animal, or higher self that makes you feel safe and loved: **Imagine** and feel this essence. Soften your gaze/or close your eyes and take a few deep breaths as you connect. **Feel** and sense the loving, caring, and safe contact. Allow yourself to **melt** into the most soothing and comforting embrace. Allow yourself to **stay here for a full minute**. Is there a **sensation** or a **message** that comes to you? **Where** do you feel it in your body? *List the words that best describe this experience:*

_____

_____

_____

Identify one thing you are **grateful** for today: Make sure it's different from what you identified yesterday. [Even the smallest things count] Soften your gaze/or close your eyes and take a few deep breaths as you **take a full minute** to **savor** this feeling of gratitude. *Write the details below:*

_____

_____

_____

Identify a current **need**. Go inside and ask yourself "what do I need?" *Write in third person "your name needs":*

_____

_____

_____

Starting My Day _____/_____/_____

Clear out some mental space. *Briefly describe the strongest thought or stressor that is on your mind – Label the emotion.*

_____

_____

_____

Body Location: _____ Body Sensation: _____

RVRR Part 1: Take a minute to perform part 1 of the RVRR technique. Now, set a plan for when, where and how you will release your vault later today. *Write your plan below:*

_____

_____

_____

Picture just one aspect of your ultimate dream life: Do not plan or strategize about how it's going to happen. **Just picture the final result.** Soften your gaze/or close your eyes and take a few deep breaths as you imagine and connect this part of your ultimate dream life. **Take a full minute** to **enjoy** this experience. How does this part of your ultimate dream life look and feel? *Write the words "What if...?" and then describe this specific aspect of your ultimate dream life.*

_____

_____

_____

_____

_____

Look deep into yourself: See and feel who you are at your core - your values, essence, innate abilities, and your heart. What images and qualities represent the real you? **Affirm** your unique personality. *List the words that best describe you:*

_____

_____

_____

_____

Ending My Day _____/_____/_____

List two things that went your way today. [Even the smallest things are good to notice]

1._____

2._____

RVRR Part 2: Did you release your vault? How did it go? *Write about it here:*
_____
_____
_____

Visualize a person, place, animal, or higher self that makes you feel safe and loved: **Imagine** and feel this essence. Soften your gaze/or close your eyes and take a few deep breaths as you connect. **Feel** and sense the loving, caring, and safe contact. Allow yourself to **melt** into the most soothing and comforting embrace. Allow yourself to **stay here for a full minute**. Is there a **sensation** or a **message** that comes to you? **Where** do you feel it in your body? *List the words that best describe this experience:*
_____
_____
_____

Identify one thing you are **grateful** for today: Make sure it's different from what you identified yesterday. [Even the smallest things count] Soften your gaze/or close your eyes and take a few deep breaths as you **take a full minute** to **savor** this feeling of gratitude. *Write the details below:*
_____
_____
_____

Identify a current **need**. Go inside and ask yourself "what do I need?" *Write in third person "your name needs":*
_____
_____

Starting My Day _____/_____/_____

Clear out some mental space. *Briefly describe the strongest thought or stressor that is on your mind – Label the emotion.*

_____

_____

_____

Body Location: _____ Body Sensation: _____

RVRR Part 1: Take a minute to perform part 1 of the RVRR technique. Now, set a plan for when, where and how you will release your vault later today. *Write your plan below:*

_____

_____

_____

Picture just one aspect of your ultimate dream life: Do not plan or strategize about how it's going to happen. **Just picture the final result.** Soften your gaze/or close your eyes and take a few deep breaths as you imagine and connect this part of your ultimate dream life. **Take a full minute** to **enjoy** this experience. How does this part of your ultimate dream life look and feel? *Write the words "What if…?" and then describe this specific aspect of your ultimate dream life.*

_____

_____

_____

_____

_____

Look deep into yourself: See and feel who you are at your core – your values, essence, innate abilities, and your heart. What images and qualities represent the real you? **Affirm** your unique personality. *List the words that best describe you:*

_____

_____

_____

_____

Ending My Day _____/_____/_____

List two things that went your way today. [Even the smallest things are good to notice]

1._____

2._____

RVRR Part 2: Did you release your vault? How did it go? *Write about it here:*
_____
_____
_____

Visualize a person, place, animal, or higher self that makes you feel safe and loved: **Imagine** and feel this essence. Soften your gaze/or close your eyes and take a few deep breaths as you connect. **Feel** and sense the loving, caring, and safe contact. Allow yourself to **melt** into the most soothing and comforting embrace. Allow yourself to **stay here for a full minute**. Is there a **sensation** or a **message** that comes to you? **Where** do you feel it in your body? *List the words that best describe this experience:*
_____
_____
_____
_____

Identify one thing you are **grateful** for today: Make sure it's different from what you identified yesterday. [Even the smallest things count] Soften your gaze/or close your eyes and take a few deep breaths as you **take a full minute** to **savor** this feeling of gratitude. *Write the details below:*
_____
_____
_____

Identify a current **need**. Go inside and ask yourself "what do I need?" *Write in third person "your name needs":*
_____
_____

Starting My Day _____/_____/_____

Clear out some mental space. *Briefly describe the strongest thought or stressor that is on your mind – Label the emotion.*

_____

_____

_____

Body Location: _____ Body Sensation: _____

RVRR Part 1: Take a minute to perform part 1 of the RVRR technique. Now, set a plan for when, where and how you will release your vault later today. *Write your plan below:*

_____

_____

_____

Picture just one aspect of your ultimate dream life: Do not plan or strategize about how it's going to happen. **Just picture the final result.** Soften your gaze/or close your eyes and take a few deep breaths as you imagine and connect this part of your ultimate dream life. **Take a full minute** to **enjoy** this experience. How does this part of your ultimate dream life look and feel? *Write the words "What if...?" and then describe this specific aspect of your ultimate dream life.*

_____

_____

_____

_____

_____

Look deep into yourself: See and feel who you are at your core - your values, essence, innate abilities, and your heart. What images and qualities represent the real you? **Affirm** your unique personality. *List the words that best describe you:*

_____

_____

_____

_____

Ending My Day _____/_____/_____

List two things that went your way today. [Even the smallest things are good to notice]

1._____
2._____

RVRR Part 2: Did you release your vault? How did it go? *Write about it here:*
_____
_____
_____

Visualize a person, place, animal, or higher self that makes you feel safe and loved: **Imagine** and feel this essence. Soften your gaze/or close your eyes and take a few deep breaths as you connect. **Feel** and sense the loving, caring, and safe contact. Allow yourself to **melt** into the most soothing and comforting embrace. Allow yourself to **stay here for a full minute.** Is there a **sensation** or a **message** that comes to you? **Where** do you feel it in your body? *List the words that best describe this experience:*
_____
_____
_____
_____

Identify one thing you are **grateful** for today: Make sure it's different from what you identified yesterday. [Even the smallest things count] Soften your gaze/or close your eyes and take a few deep breaths as you **take a full minute** to **savor** this feeling of gratitude. *Write the details below:*
_____
_____
_____

Identify a current **need**. Go inside and ask yourself "what do I need?" *Write in third person "your name needs":*
_____
_____
_____

Starting My Day _____/_____/_____

Clear out some mental space. *Briefly describe the strongest thought or stressor that is on your mind – Label the emotion.*

_____

_____

_____

Body Location: _____ Body Sensation: _____

RVRR Part 1: Take a minute to perform part 1 of the RVRR technique. Now, set a plan for when, where and how you will release your vault later today. *Write your plan below:*

_____

_____

_____

Picture just one aspect of your ultimate dream life: Do not plan or strategize about how it's going to happen. **Just picture the final result**. Soften your gaze/or close your eyes and take a few deep breaths as you imagine and connect this part of your ultimate dream life. **Take a full minute** to **enjoy** this experience. How does this part of your ultimate dream life look and feel? *Write the words "What if…?" and then describe this specific aspect of your ultimate dream life.*

_____

_____

_____

_____

_____

Look deep into yourself: See and feel who you are at your core - your values, essence, innate abilities, and your heart. What images and qualities represent the real you? **Affirm** your unique personality. *List the words that best describe you:*

_____

_____

_____

_____

Ending My Day _____/_____/_____

List two things that went your way today. [Even the smallest things are good to notice]

1._____

2._____

RVRR Part 2: Did you release your vault? How did it go? *Write about it here:*
_____
_____
_____

Visualize a person, place, animal, or higher self that makes you feel safe and loved: **Imagine** and feel this essence. Soften your gaze/or close your eyes and take a few deep breaths as you connect. **Feel** and sense the loving, caring, and safe contact. Allow yourself to **melt** into the most soothing and comforting embrace. Allow yourself to **stay here for a full minute.** Is there a **sensation** or a **message** that comes to you? **Where** do you feel it in your body? *List the words that best describe this experience:*
_____
_____
_____
_____

Identify one thing you are **grateful** for today: Make sure it's different from what you identified yesterday. [Even the smallest things count] Soften your gaze/or close your eyes and take a few deep breaths as you **take a full minute** to **savor** this feeling of gratitude. *Write the details below:*
_____
_____
_____

Identify a current **need**. Go inside and ask yourself "what do I need?" *Write in third person "your name needs":*
_____
_____
_____

Starting My Day _____/_____/_____

Clear out some mental space. *Briefly describe the strongest thought or stressor that is on your mind – Label the emotion.*

_____
_____
_____

Body Location: _____ Body Sensation: _____

RVRR Part 1: Take a minute to perform part 1 of the RVRR technique. Now, set a plan for when, where and how you will release your vault later today. *Write your plan below:*

_____
_____
_____

Picture just one aspect of your ultimate dream life: Do not plan or strategize about how it's going to happen. **Just picture the final result.** Soften your gaze/or close your eyes and take a few deep breaths as you imagine and connect this part of your ultimate dream life. **Take a full minute** to **enjoy** this experience. How does this part of your ultimate dream life look and feel? *Write the words "What if...?" and then describe this specific aspect of your ultimate dream life.*

_____
_____
_____
_____
_____

Look deep into yourself: See and feel who you are at your core - your values, essence, innate abilities, and your heart. What images and qualities represent the real you? **Affirm** your unique personality. *List the words that best describe you:*

_____
_____
_____
_____
_____

@QuantumMindframe

Ending My Day _____/_____/_____

List two things that went your way today. [Even the smallest things are good to notice]

1._____

2._____

RVRR Part 2: Did you release your vault? How did it go? *Write about it here:*
_____
_____
_____

Visualize a person, place, animal, or higher self that makes you feel safe and loved: **Imagine** and feel this essence. Soften your gaze/or close your eyes and take a few deep breaths as you connect. **Feel** and sense the loving, caring, and safe contact. Allow yourself to **melt** into the most soothing and comforting embrace. Allow yourself to **stay here for a full minute**. Is there a **sensation** or a **message** that comes to you? **Where** do you feel it in your body? *List the words that best describe this experience:*
_____
_____
_____

Identify one thing you are **grateful** for today: Make sure it's different from what you identified yesterday. [Even the smallest things count] Soften your gaze/or close your eyes and take a few deep breaths as you **take a full minute** to **savor** this feeling of gratitude. *Write the details below:*
_____
_____
_____

Identify a current **need**. Go inside and ask yourself "what do I need?" *Write in third person "your name needs":*
_____
_____

Starting My Day _____/_____/_____

Clear out some mental space. *Briefly describe the strongest thought or stressor that is on your mind – Label the emotion.*

_____
_____
_____

Body Location: _____ Body Sensation: _____

RVRR Part 1: Take a minute to perform part 1 of the RVRR technique. Now, set a plan for when, where and how you will release your vault later today. *Write your plan below:*

_____
_____
_____

Picture just one aspect of your ultimate dream life: Do not plan or strategize about how it's going to happen. **Just picture the final result.** Soften your gaze/or close your eyes and take a few deep breaths as you imagine and connect this part of your ultimate dream life. **Take a full minute** to **enjoy** this experience. How does this part of your ultimate dream life look and feel? *Write the words "What if...?" and then describe this specific aspect of your ultimate dream life.*

_____
_____
_____
_____
_____

Look deep into yourself: See and feel who you are at your core - your values, essence, innate abilities, and your heart. What images and qualities represent the real you? **Affirm** your unique personality. *List the words that best describe you:*

_____
_____
_____
_____

Ending My Day _____/_____/_____

List two things that went your way today. [Even the smallest things are good to notice]

1._____

2._____

RVRR Part 2: Did you release your vault? How did it go? *Write about it here:*

_____

_____

Visualize a person, place, animal, or higher self that makes you feel safe and loved: **Imagine** and feel this essence. Soften your gaze/or close your eyes and take a few deep breaths as you connect. **Feel** and sense the loving, caring, and safe contact. Allow yourself to **melt** into the most soothing and comforting embrace. Allow yourself to **stay here for a full minute**. Is there a **sensation** or a **message** that comes to you? **Where** do you feel it in your body? *List the words that best describe this experience:*

_____

_____

_____

Identify one thing you are **grateful** for today: Make sure it's different from what you identified yesterday. [Even the smallest things count] Soften your gaze/or close your eyes and take a few deep breaths as you **take a full minute** to **savor** this feeling of gratitude. *Write the details below:*

_____

_____

Identify a current **need**. Go inside and ask yourself "what do I need?" *Write in third person "your name needs":*

_____

_____

Starting My Day _____/_____/_____

Clear out some mental space. *Briefly describe the strongest thought or stressor that is on your mind – Label the emotion.*

_____

_____

_____

Body Location: _____ Body Sensation: _____

RVRR Part 1: Take a minute to perform part 1 of the RVRR technique. Now, set a plan for when, where and how you will release your vault later today. *Write your plan below:*

_____

_____

_____

Picture just one aspect of your ultimate dream life: Do not plan or strategize about how it's going to happen. **Just picture the final result**. Soften your gaze/or close your eyes and take a few deep breaths as you imagine and connect this part of your ultimate dream life. **Take a full minute** to **enjoy** this experience. How does this part of your ultimate dream life look and feel? *Write the words "What if...?" and then describe this specific aspect of your ultimate dream life.*

_____

_____

_____

_____

_____

Look deep into yourself: See and feel who you are at your core - your values, essence, innate abilities, and your heart. What images and qualities represent the real you? **Affirm** your unique personality. *List the words that best describe you:*

_____

_____

_____

_____

_____

Ending My Day _____/_____/_____

List two things that went your way today. [Even the smallest things are good to notice]

1. _____

2. _____

RVRR Part 2: Did you release your vault? How did it go? *Write about it here:*

_____

_____

_____

Visualize a person, place, animal, or higher self that makes you feel safe and loved: **Imagine** and feel this essence. Soften your gaze/or close your eyes and take a few deep breaths as you connect. **Feel** and sense the loving, caring, and safe contact. Allow yourself to **melt** into the most soothing and comforting embrace. Allow yourself to **stay here for a full minute**. Is there a **sensation** or a **message** that comes to you? **Where** do you feel it in your body? *List the words that best describe this experience:*

_____

_____

_____

Identify one thing you are **grateful** for today: Make sure it's different from what you identified yesterday. [Even the smallest things count] Soften your gaze/or close your eyes and take a few deep breaths as you **take a full minute** to **savor** this feeling of gratitude. *Write the details below:*

_____

_____

_____

Identify a current **need**. Go inside and ask yourself "what do I need?" *Write in third person "your name needs":*

_____

_____

_____

Starting My Day _____/_____/_____

Clear out some mental space. *Briefly describe the strongest thought or stressor that is on your mind – Label the emotion.*

_____
_____
_____

Body Location: _____ Body Sensation: _____

RVRR Part 1: Take a minute to perform part 1 of the RVRR technique. Now, set a plan for when, where and how you will release your vault later today. *Write your plan below:*

_____
_____
_____

Picture just one aspect of your ultimate dream life: Do not plan or strategize about how it's going to happen. **Just picture the final result.** Soften your gaze/or close your eyes and take a few deep breaths as you imagine and connect this part of your ultimate dream life. **Take a full minute** to **enjoy** this experience. How does this part of your ultimate dream life look and feel? *Write the words "What if...?" and then describe this specific aspect of your ultimate dream life.*

_____
_____
_____
_____

Look deep into yourself: See and feel who you are at your core - your values, essence, innate abilities, and your heart. What images and qualities represent the real you? **Affirm** your unique personality. *List the words that best describe you:*

_____
_____
_____
_____

@QuantumMindframe

Ending My Day _____ / _____ / _____

List two things that went your way today. [Even the smallest things are good to notice]

1. _____
2. _____

RVRR Part 2: Did you release your vault? How did it go? *Write about it here:*

_____
_____
_____

Visualize a person, place, animal, or higher self that makes you feel safe and loved: **Imagine** and feel this essence. Soften your gaze/or close your eyes and take a few deep breaths as you connect. **Feel** and sense the loving, caring, and safe contact. Allow yourself to **melt** into the most soothing and comforting embrace. Allow yourself to **stay here for a full minute**. Is there a **sensation** or a **message** that comes to you? **Where** do you feel it in your body? *List the words that best describe this experience:*

_____
_____
_____
_____

Identify one thing you are **grateful** for today: Make sure it's different from what you identified yesterday. [Even the smallest things count] Soften your gaze/or close your eyes and take a few deep breaths as you **take a full minute** to **savor** this feeling of gratitude. *Write the details below:*

_____
_____
_____

Identify a current **need**. Go inside and ask yourself "what do I need?" *Write in third person "your name needs":*

_____
_____
_____

Starting My Day _____/_____/_____

Clear out some mental space. *Briefly describe the strongest thought or stressor that is on your mind – Label the emotion.*

_____

_____

_____

Body Location: _____ Body Sensation: _____

RVRR Part 1: Take a minute to perform part 1 of the RVRR technique. Now, set a plan for when, where and how you will release your vault later today. *Write your plan below:*

_____

_____

_____

Picture just one aspect of your ultimate dream life: Do not plan or strategize about how it's going to happen. **Just picture the final result**. Soften your gaze/or close your eyes and take a few deep breaths as you imagine and connect this part of your ultimate dream life. **Take a full minute** to **enjoy** this experience. How does this part of your ultimate dream life look and feel? *Write the words "What if…?" and then describe this specific aspect of your ultimate dream life.*

_____

_____

_____

_____

_____

Look deep into yourself: See and feel who you are at your core - your values, essence, innate abilities, and your heart. What images and qualities represent the real you? **Affirm** your unique personality. *List the words that best describe you:*

_____

_____

_____

_____

Ending My Day _____/_____/_____

List two things that went your way today. [Even the smallest things are good to notice]

1._____

2._____

RVRR Part 2: Did you release your vault? How did it go? *Write about it here:*
_____
_____
_____

Visualize a person, place, animal, or higher self that makes you feel safe and loved: **Imagine** and feel this essence. Soften your gaze/or close your eyes and take a few deep breaths as you connect. **Feel** and sense the loving, caring, and safe contact. Allow yourself to **melt** into the most soothing and comforting embrace. Allow yourself to **stay here for a full minute**. Is there a **sensation** or a **message** that comes to you? **Where** do you feel it in your body? *List the words that best describe this experience:*
_____
_____
_____

Identify one thing you are **grateful** for today: Make sure it's different from what you identified yesterday. [Even the smallest things count] Soften your gaze/or close your eyes and take a few deep breaths as you **take a full minute** to **savor** this feeling of gratitude. *Write the details below:*
_____
_____
_____

Identify a current **need**. Go inside and ask yourself "what do I need?" *Write in third person "your name needs":*
_____
_____
_____

Starting My Day _____/_____/_____

Clear out some mental space. *Briefly describe the strongest thought or stressor that is on your mind – Label the emotion.*

_____

_____

_____

Body Location: _____ Body Sensation: _____

RVRR Part 1: Take a minute to perform part 1 of the RVRR technique. Now, set a plan for when, where and how you will release your vault later today. *Write your plan below:*

_____

_____

_____

Picture just one aspect of your ultimate dream life: Do not plan or strategize about how it's going to happen. **Just picture the final result.** Soften your gaze/or close your eyes and take a few deep breaths as you imagine and connect this part of your ultimate dream life. **Take a full minute** to **enjoy** this experience. How does this part of your ultimate dream life look and feel? *Write the words "What if...?" and then describe this specific aspect of your ultimate dream life.*

_____

_____

_____

_____

_____

Look deep into yourself: See and feel who you are at your core - your values, essence, innate abilities, and your heart. What images and qualities represent the real you? **Affirm** your unique personality. *List the words that best describe you:*

_____

_____

_____

_____

Ending My Day _____/_____/_____

List two things that went your way today. [Even the smallest things are good to notice]

1._____

2._____

RVRR Part 2: Did you release your vault? How did it go? *Write about it here:*

_____
_____

Visualize a person, place, animal, or higher self that makes you feel safe and loved: **Imagine** and feel this essence. Soften your gaze/or close your eyes and take a few deep breaths as you connect. **Feel** and sense the loving, caring, and safe contact. Allow yourself to **melt** into the most soothing and comforting embrace. Allow yourself to **stay here for a full minute**. Is there a **sensation** or a **message** that comes to you? **Where** do you feel it in your body? *List the words that best describe this experience:*

_____
_____
_____

Identify one thing you are **grateful** for today: Make sure it's different from what you identified yesterday. [Even the smallest things count] Soften your gaze/or close your eyes and take a few deep breaths as you **take a full minute** to **savor** this feeling of gratitude. *Write the details below:*

_____
_____
_____

Identify a current **need**. Go inside and ask yourself "what do I need?" *Write in third person "your name needs":*

_____
_____
_____

Starting My Day _____/_____/_____

Clear out some mental space. *Briefly describe the strongest thought or stressor that is on your mind – Label the emotion.*

_____

_____

_____

Body Location: _____ Body Sensation: _____

RVRR Part 1: Take a minute to perform part 1 of the RVRR technique. Now, set a plan for when, where and how you will release your vault later today. *Write your plan below:*

_____

_____

_____

Picture just one aspect of your ultimate dream life: Do not plan or strategize about how it's going to happen. **Just picture the final result.** Soften your gaze/or close your eyes and take a few deep breaths as you imagine and connect this part of your ultimate dream life. **Take a full minute** to **enjoy** this experience. How does this part of your ultimate dream life look and feel? *Write the words "What if…?" and then describe this specific aspect of your ultimate dream life.*

_____

_____

_____

_____

_____

Look deep into yourself: See and feel who you are at your core - your values, essence, innate abilities, and your heart. What images and qualities represent the real you? **Affirm** your unique personality. *List the words that best describe you:*

_____

_____

_____

_____

Ending My Day _____/_____/_____

List two things that went your way today. [Even the smallest things are good to notice]

1._____

2._____

RVRR Part 2: Did you release your vault? How did it go? *Write about it here:*
_____
_____

Visualize a person, place, animal, or higher self that makes you feel safe and loved: **Imagine** and feel this essence. Soften your gaze/or close your eyes and take a few deep breaths as you connect. **Feel** and sense the loving, caring, and safe contact. Allow yourself to **melt** into the most soothing and comforting embrace. Allow yourself to **stay here for a full minute**. Is there a **sensation** or a **message** that comes to you? **Where** do you feel it in your body? *List the words that best describe this experience:*
_____
_____
_____

Identify one thing you are **grateful** for today: Make sure it's different from what you identified yesterday. [Even the smallest things count] Soften your gaze/or close your eyes and take a few deep breaths as you **take a full minute** to **savor** this feeling of gratitude. *Write the details below:*
_____
_____
_____

Identify a current **need**. Go inside and ask yourself "what do I need?" *Write in third person "your name needs":*
_____
_____
_____

Starting My Day _____/_____/_____

Clear out some mental space. *Briefly describe the strongest thought or stressor that is on your mind – Label the emotion.*

_____

_____

_____

Body Location: _____ Body Sensation: _____

RVRR Part 1: Take a minute to perform part 1 of the RVRR technique. Now, set a plan for when, where and how you will release your vault later today. *Write your plan below:*

_____

_____

_____

Picture just one aspect of your ultimate dream life: Do not plan or strategize about how it's going to happen. **Just picture the final result**. Soften your gaze/or close your eyes and take a few deep breaths as you imagine and connect this part of your ultimate dream life. **Take a full minute** to **enjoy** this experience. How does this part of your ultimate dream life look and feel? *Write the words "What if…?" and then describe this specific aspect of your ultimate dream life.*

_____

_____

_____

_____

_____

Look deep into yourself: See and feel who you are at your core - your values, essence, innate abilities, and your heart. What images and qualities represent the real you? **Affirm** your unique personality. *List the words that best describe you:*

_____

_____

_____

_____

_____

@QuantumMindframe

Ending My Day _____/_____/_____

List two things that went your way today. [Even the smallest things are good to notice]

1._____

2._____

RVRR Part 2: Did you release your vault? How did it go? *Write about it here:*
_____
_____
_____

Visualize a person, place, animal, or higher self that makes you feel safe and loved: **Imagine** and feel this essence. Soften your gaze/or close your eyes and take a few deep breaths as you connect. **Feel** and sense the loving, caring, and safe contact. Allow yourself to **melt** into the most soothing and comforting embrace. Allow yourself to **stay here for a full minute**. Is there a **sensation** or a **message** that comes to you? **Where** do you feel it in your body? *List the words that best describe this experience:*
_____
_____
_____
_____

Identify one thing you are **grateful** for today: Make sure it's different from what you identified yesterday. [Even the smallest things count] Soften your gaze/or close your eyes and take a few deep breaths as you **take a full minute** to **savor** this feeling of gratitude. *Write the details below:*
_____
_____
_____

Identify a current **need**. Go inside and ask yourself "what do I need?" *Write in third person "your name needs":*
_____
_____
_____

Starting My Day _____/_____/_____

Clear out some mental space. *Briefly describe the strongest thought or stressor that is on your mind – Label the emotion.*

_____

_____

_____

Body Location: _____ Body Sensation: _____

RVRR Part 1: Take a minute to perform part 1 of the RVRR technique. Now, set a plan for when, where and how you will release your vault later today. *Write your plan below:*

_____

_____

_____

Picture just one aspect of your ultimate dream life: Do not plan or strategize about how it's going to happen. **Just picture the final result**. Soften your gaze/or close your eyes and take a few deep breaths as you imagine and connect this part of your ultimate dream life. **Take a full minute** to **enjoy** this experience. How does this part of your ultimate dream life look and feel? *Write the words "What if...?" and then describe this specific aspect of your ultimate dream life.*

_____

_____

_____

_____

_____

Look deep into yourself: See and feel who you are at your core - your values, essence, innate abilities, and your heart. What images and qualities represent the real you? **Affirm** your unique personality. *List the words that best describe you:*

_____

_____

_____

_____

Ending My Day _____/_____/_____

List two things that went your way today. [Even the smallest things are good to notice]

1._____

2._____

RVRR Part 2: Did you release your vault? How did it go? *Write about it here:*

_____

_____

Visualize a person, place, animal, or higher self that makes you feel safe and loved: **Imagine** and feel this essence. Soften your gaze/or close your eyes and take a few deep breaths as you connect. **Feel** and sense the loving, caring, and safe contact. Allow yourself to **melt** into the most soothing and comforting embrace. Allow yourself to **stay here for a full minute**. Is there a **sensation** or a **message** that comes to you? **Where** do you feel it in your body? *List the words that best describe this experience:*

_____

_____

_____

Identify one thing you are **grateful** for today: Make sure it's different from what you identified yesterday. [Even the smallest things count] Soften your gaze/or close your eyes and take a few deep breaths as you **take a full minute** to **savor** this feeling of gratitude. *Write the details below:*

_____

_____

_____

Identify a current **need**. Go inside and ask yourself "what do I need?" *Write in third person "your name needs":*

_____

_____

_____

Starting My Day _____/_____/_____

Clear out some mental space. *Briefly describe the strongest thought or stressor that is on your mind – Label the emotion.*

_____
_____
_____

Body Location: _____ Body Sensation: _____

RVRR Part 1: Take a minute to perform part 1 of the RVRR technique. Now, set a plan for when, where and how you will release your vault later today. *Write your plan below:*

_____
_____
_____

Picture just one aspect of your ultimate dream life: Do not plan or strategize about how it's going to happen. **Just picture the final result.** Soften your gaze/or close your eyes and take a few deep breaths as you imagine and connect this part of your ultimate dream life. **Take a full minute** to **enjoy** this experience. How does this part of your ultimate dream life look and feel? *Write the words "What if...?" and then describe this specific aspect of your ultimate dream life.*

_____
_____
_____
_____
_____

Look deep into yourself: See and feel who you are at your core - your values, essence, innate abilities, and your heart. What images and qualities represent the real you? **Affirm** your unique personality. *List the words that best describe you:*

_____
_____
_____
_____

Ending My Day _____/_____/_____

List two things that went your way today. [Even the smallest things are good to notice]

1._____

2._____

RVRR Part 2: Did you release your vault? How did it go? *Write about it here:*
_____
_____
_____

Visualize a person, place, animal, or higher self that makes you feel safe and loved: **Imagine** and feel this essence. Soften your gaze/or close your eyes and take a few deep breaths as you connect. **Feel** and sense the loving, caring, and safe contact. Allow yourself to **melt** into the most soothing and comforting embrace. Allow yourself to **stay here for a full minute**. Is there a **sensation** or a **message** that comes to you? **Where** do you feel it in your body? *List the words that best describe this experience:*
_____
_____
_____

Identify one thing you are **grateful** for today: Make sure it's different from what you identified yesterday. [Even the smallest things count] Soften your gaze/or close your eyes and take a few deep breaths as you **take a full minute** to **savor** this feeling of gratitude. *Write the details below:*
_____
_____
_____

Identify a current **need**. Go inside and ask yourself "what do I need?" *Write in third person "your name needs":*
_____
_____
_____

Starting My Day _____/_____/_____

Clear out some mental space. *Briefly describe the strongest thought or stressor that is on your mind – Label the emotion.*

_____

_____

_____

Body Location: _____ Body Sensation: _____

RVRR Part 1: Take a minute to perform part 1 of the RVRR technique. Now, set a plan for when, where and how you will release your vault later today. *Write your plan below:*

_____

_____

_____

Picture just one aspect of your ultimate dream life: Do not plan or strategize about how it's going to happen. **Just picture the final result**. Soften your gaze/or close your eyes and take a few deep breaths as you imagine and connect this part of your ultimate dream life. **Take a full minute** to **enjoy** this experience. How does this part of your ultimate dream life look and feel? *Write the words "What if…?" and then describe this specific aspect of your ultimate dream life.*

_____

_____

_____

_____

_____

Look deep into yourself: See and feel who you are at your core - your values, essence, innate abilities, and your heart. What images and qualities represent the real you? **Affirm** your unique personality. *List the words that best describe you:*

_____

_____

_____

_____

Ending My Day _____/_____/_____

List two things that went your way today. [Even the smallest things are good to notice]

1._____

2._____

RVRR Part 2: Did you release your vault? How did it go? *Write about it here:*

_____

_____

_____

Visualize a person, place, animal, or higher self that makes you feel safe and loved: **Imagine** and feel this essence. Soften your gaze/or close your eyes and take a few deep breaths as you connect. **Feel** and sense the loving, caring, and safe contact. Allow yourself to **melt** into the most soothing and comforting embrace. Allow yourself to **stay here for a full minute**. Is there a **sensation** or a **message** that comes to you? **Where** do you feel it in your body? *List the words that best describe this experience:*

_____

_____

_____

_____

Identify one thing you are **grateful** for today: Make sure it's different from what you identified yesterday. [Even the smallest things count] Soften your gaze/or close your eyes and take a few deep breaths as you **take a full minute** to **savor** this feeling of gratitude. *Write the details below:*

_____

_____

_____

Identify a current **need**. Go inside and ask yourself "what do I need?" *Write in third person "your name needs":*

_____

_____

_____

Starting My Day _____/_____/_____

Clear out some mental space. *Briefly describe the strongest thought or stressor that is on your mind – Label the emotion.*

_____

_____

_____

Body Location: _____ Body Sensation: _____

RVRR Part 1: Take a minute to perform part 1 of the RVRR technique. Now, set a plan for when, where and how you will release your vault later today. *Write your plan below:*

_____

_____

_____

Picture just one aspect of your ultimate dream life: Do not plan or strategize about how it's going to happen. **Just picture the final result.** Soften your gaze/or close your eyes and take a few deep breaths as you imagine and connect this part of your ultimate dream life. **Take a full minute** to **enjoy** this experience. How does this part of your ultimate dream life look and feel? *Write the words "What if…?" and then describe this specific aspect of your ultimate dream life.*

_____

_____

_____

_____

_____

Look deep into yourself: See and feel who you are at your core - your values, essence, innate abilities, and your heart. What images and qualities represent the real you? **Affirm** your unique personality. *List the words that best describe you:*

_____

_____

_____

_____

Ending My Day _____/_____/_____

List two things that went your way today. [Even the smallest things are good to notice]

1._____

2._____

RVRR Part 2: Did you release your vault? How did it go? *Write about it here:*
_____
_____
_____

Visualize a person, place, animal, or higher self that makes you feel safe and loved: **Imagine** and feel this essence. Soften your gaze/or close your eyes and take a few deep breaths as you connect. **Feel** and sense the loving, caring, and safe contact. Allow yourself to **melt** into the most soothing and comforting embrace. Allow yourself to **stay here for a full minute**. Is there a **sensation** or a **message** that comes to you? **Where** do you feel it in your body? *List the words that best describe this experience:*
_____
_____
_____
_____

Identify one thing you are **grateful** for today: Make sure it's different from what you identified yesterday. [Even the smallest things count] Soften your gaze/or close your eyes and take a few deep breaths as you **take a full minute** to **savor** this feeling of gratitude. *Write the details below:*
_____
_____
_____

Identify a current **need**. Go inside and ask yourself "what do I need?" *Write in third person "your name needs":*
_____
_____
_____

Starting My Day _____/_____/_____

Clear out some mental space. *Briefly describe the strongest thought or stressor that is on your mind – Label the emotion.*

_____

_____

_____

Body Location: _____ Body Sensation: _____

RVRR Part 1: Take a minute to perform part 1 of the RVRR technique. Now, set a plan for when, where and how you will release your vault later today. *Write your plan below:*

_____

_____

_____

Picture just one aspect of your ultimate dream life: Do not plan or strategize about how it's going to happen. **Just picture the final result.** Soften your gaze/or close your eyes and take a few deep breaths as you imagine and connect this part of your ultimate dream life. **Take a full minute** to **enjoy** this experience. How does this part of your ultimate dream life look and feel? *Write the words "What if…?" and then describe this specific aspect of your ultimate dream life.*

_____

_____

_____

_____

_____

_____

Look deep into yourself: See and feel who you are at your core - your values, essence, innate abilities, and your heart. What images and qualities represent the real you? **Affirm** your unique personality. *List the words that best describe you:*

_____

_____

_____

_____

Ending My Day _____/_____/_____

List two things that went your way today. [Even the smallest things are good to notice]

1._____

2._____

RVRR Part 2: Did you release your vault? How did it go? *Write about it here:*

_____

_____

Visualize a person, place, animal, or higher self that makes you feel safe and loved: **Imagine** and feel this essence. Soften your gaze/or close your eyes and take a few deep breaths as you connect. **Feel** and sense the loving, caring, and safe contact. Allow yourself to **melt** into the most soothing and comforting embrace. Allow yourself to **stay here for a full minute.** Is there a **sensation** or a **message** that comes to you? **Where** do you feel it in your body? *List the words that best describe this experience:*

_____

_____

_____

Identify one thing you are **grateful** for today: Make sure it's different from what you identified yesterday. [Even the smallest things count] Soften your gaze/or close your eyes and take a few deep breaths as you **take a full minute** to **savor** this feeling of gratitude. *Write the details below:*

_____

_____

_____

Identify a current **need**. Go inside and ask yourself "what do I need?" *Write in third person "your name needs":*

_____

_____

_____

Starting My Day _____/_____/_____

Clear out some mental space. *Briefly describe the strongest thought or stressor that is on your mind – Label the emotion.*

_____

_____

_____

Body Location: _____ Body Sensation: _____

RVRR Part 1: Take a minute to perform part 1 of the RVRR technique. Now, set a plan for when, where and how you will release your vault later today. *Write your plan below:*

_____

_____

_____

Picture just one aspect of your ultimate dream life: Do not plan or strategize about how it's going to happen. **Just picture the final result**. Soften your gaze/or close your eyes and take a few deep breaths as you imagine and connect this part of your ultimate dream life. **Take a full minute** to **enjoy** this experience. How does this part of your ultimate dream life look and feel? *Write the words "What if…?" and then describe this specific aspect of your ultimate dream life.*

_____

_____

_____

_____

_____

Look deep into yourself: See and feel who you are at your core - your values, essence, innate abilities, and your heart. What images and qualities represent the real you? **Affirm** your unique personality. *List the words that best describe you:*

_____

_____

_____

_____

Ending My Day _____/_____/_____

List two things that went your way today. [Even the smallest things are good to notice]

1._____

2._____

RVRR Part 2: Did you release your vault? How did it go? *Write about it here:*
_____
_____
_____

Visualize a person, place, animal, or higher self that makes you feel safe and loved: **Imagine** and feel this essence. Soften your gaze/or close your eyes and take a few deep breaths as you connect. **Feel** and sense the loving, caring, and safe contact. Allow yourself to **melt** into the most soothing and comforting embrace. Allow yourself to **stay here for a full minute**. Is there a **sensation** or a **message** that comes to you? **Where** do you feel it in your body? *List the words that best describe this experience:*
_____
_____
_____
_____

Identify one thing you are **grateful** for today: Make sure it's different from what you identified yesterday. [Even the smallest things count] Soften your gaze/or close your eyes and take a few deep breaths as you **take a full minute** to **savor** this feeling of gratitude. *Write the details below:*
_____
_____
_____

Identify a current **need**. Go inside and ask yourself "what do I need?" *Write in third person "your name needs":*
_____
_____
_____

Starting My Day _____/_____/_____

Clear out some mental space. *Briefly describe the strongest thought or stressor that is on your mind – Label the emotion.*

_____

_____

_____

Body Location: _____ Body Sensation: _____

RVRR Part 1: Take a minute to perform part 1 of the RVRR technique. Now, set a plan for when, where and how you will release your vault later today. *Write your plan below:*

_____

_____

_____

Picture just one aspect of your ultimate dream life: Do not plan or strategize about how it's going to happen. **Just picture the final result**. Soften your gaze/or close your eyes and take a few deep breaths as you imagine and connect this part of your ultimate dream life. **Take a full minute** to **enjoy** this experience. How does this part of your ultimate dream life look and feel? *Write the words "What if…?" and then describe this specific aspect of your ultimate dream life.*

_____

_____

_____

_____

_____

Look deep into yourself: See and feel who you are at your core - your values, essence, innate abilities, and your heart. What images and qualities represent the real you? **Affirm** your unique personality. *List the words that best describe you:*

_____

_____

_____

_____

Ending My Day _____/_____/_____

List two things that went your way today. [Even the smallest things are good to notice]

1._____

2._____

RVRR Part 2: Did you release your vault? How did it go? *Write about it here:*
_____
_____

Visualize a person, place, animal, or higher self that makes you feel safe and loved: **Imagine** and feel this essence. Soften your gaze/or close your eyes and take a few deep breaths as you connect. **Feel** and sense the loving, caring, and safe contact. Allow yourself to **melt** into the most soothing and comforting embrace. Allow yourself to **stay here for a full minute**. Is there a **sensation** or a **message** that comes to you? **Where** do you feel it in your body? *List the words that best describe this experience:*
_____
_____
_____
_____

Identify one thing you are **grateful** for today: Make sure it's different from what you identified yesterday. [Even the smallest things count] Soften your gaze/or close your eyes and take a few deep breaths as you **take a full minute** to **savor** this feeling of gratitude. *Write the details below:*
_____
_____
_____

Identify a current **need**. Go inside and ask yourself "what do I need?" *Write in third person "your name needs":*
_____
_____
_____

Starting My Day _____/_____/_____

Clear out some mental space. *Briefly describe the strongest thought or stressor that is on your mind – Label the emotion.*

_____

_____

_____

Body Location: _____ Body Sensation: _____

RVRR Part 1: Take a minute to perform part 1 of the RVRR technique. Now, set a plan for when, where and how you will release your vault later today. *Write your plan below:*

_____

_____

_____

Picture just one aspect of your ultimate dream life: Do not plan or strategize about how it's going to happen. **Just picture the final result**. Soften your gaze/or close your eyes and take a few deep breaths as you imagine and connect this part of your ultimate dream life. **Take a full minute** to **enjoy** this experience. How does this part of your ultimate dream life look and feel? *Write the words "What if…?" and then describe this specific aspect of your ultimate dream life.*

_____

_____

_____

_____

_____

Look deep into yourself: See and feel who you are at your core - your values, essence, innate abilities, and your heart. What images and qualities represent the real you? **Affirm** your unique personality. *List the words that best describe you:*

_____

_____

_____

_____

Ending My Day _____/_____/_____

List two things that went your way today. [Even the smallest things are good to notice]

1._____

2._____

RVRR Part 2: Did you release your vault? How did it go? *Write about it here:*
_____
_____
_____

Visualize a person, place, animal, or higher self that makes you feel safe and loved: **Imagine** and feel this essence. Soften your gaze/or close your eyes and take a few deep breaths as you connect. **Feel** and sense the loving, caring, and safe contact. Allow yourself to **melt** into the most soothing and comforting embrace. Allow yourself to **stay here for a full minute**. Is there a **sensation** or a **message** that comes to you? **Where** do you feel it in your body? *List the words that best describe this experience:*
_____
_____
_____
_____

Identify one thing you are **grateful** for today: Make sure it's different from what you identified yesterday. [Even the smallest things count] Soften your gaze/or close your eyes and take a few deep breaths as you **take a full minute** to **savor** this feeling of gratitude. *Write the details below:*
_____
_____
_____

Identify a current **need**. Go inside and ask yourself "what do I need?" *Write in third person "your name needs":*
_____
_____
_____

Starting My Day _____ / _____ / _____

Clear out some mental space. *Briefly describe the strongest thought or stressor that is on your mind – Label the emotion.*

_____

_____

_____

Body Location: _____ Body Sensation: _____

RVRR Part 1: Take a minute to perform part 1 of the RVRR technique. Now, set a plan for when, where and how you will release your vault later today. *Write your plan below:*

_____

_____

_____

Picture just one aspect of your ultimate dream life: Do not plan or strategize about how it's going to happen. **Just picture the final result**. Soften your gaze/or close your eyes and take a few deep breaths as you imagine and connect this part of your ultimate dream life. **Take a full minute** to **enjoy** this experience. How does this part of your ultimate dream life look and feel? *Write the words "What if...?" and then describe this specific aspect of your ultimate dream life.*

_____

_____

_____

_____

_____

Look deep into yourself: See and feel who you are at your core - your values, essence, innate abilities, and your heart. What images and qualities represent the real you? **Affirm** your unique personality. *List the words that best describe you:*

_____

_____

_____

_____

Ending My Day _____/_____/_____

List two things that went your way today. [Even the smallest things are good to notice]

1._____

2._____

RVRR Part 2: Did you release your vault? How did it go? *Write about it here:*
_____
_____

Visualize a person, place, animal, or higher self that makes you feel safe and loved: **Imagine** and feel this essence. Soften your gaze/or close your eyes and take a few deep breaths as you connect. **Feel** and sense the loving, caring, and safe contact. Allow yourself to **melt** into the most soothing and comforting embrace. Allow yourself to **stay here for a full minute.** Is there a **sensation** or a **message** that comes to you? **Where** do you feel it in your body? *List the words that best describe this experience:*
_____
_____
_____

Identify one thing you are **grateful** for today: Make sure it's different from what you identified yesterday. [Even the smallest things count] Soften your gaze/or close your eyes and take a few deep breaths as you **take a full minute** to **savor** this feeling of gratitude. *Write the details below:*
_____
_____
_____

Identify a current **need**. Go inside and ask yourself "what do I need?" *Write in third person "your name needs":*
_____
_____

Starting My Day _____/_____/_____

Clear out some mental space. *Briefly describe the strongest thought or stressor that is on your mind – Label the emotion.*

_____

_____

_____

Body Location: _____ Body Sensation: _____

RVRR Part 1: Take a minute to perform part 1 of the RVRR technique. Now, set a plan for when, where and how you will release your vault later today. *Write your plan below:*

_____

_____

_____

Picture just one aspect of your ultimate dream life: Do not plan or strategize about how it's going to happen. **Just picture the final result.** Soften your gaze/or close your eyes and take a few deep breaths as you imagine and connect this part of your ultimate dream life. **Take a full minute** to **enjoy** this experience. How does this part of your ultimate dream life look and feel? *Write the words "What if...?" and then describe this specific aspect of your ultimate dream life.*

_____

_____

_____

_____

_____

Look deep into yourself: See and feel who you are at your core - your values, essence, innate abilities, and your heart. What images and qualities represent the real you? **Affirm** your unique personality. *List the words that best describe you:*

_____

_____

_____

_____

_____

Ending My Day _____/_____/_____

List two things that went your way today. [Even the smallest things are good to notice]

1._____

2._____

RVRR Part 2: Did you release your vault? How did it go? *Write about it here:*
_____
_____
_____

Visualize a person, place, animal, or higher self that makes you feel safe and loved: **Imagine** and feel this essence. Soften your gaze/or close your eyes and take a few deep breaths as you connect. **Feel** and sense the loving, caring, and safe contact. Allow yourself to **melt** into the most soothing and comforting embrace. Allow yourself to **stay here for a full minute**. Is there a **sensation** or a **message** that comes to you? **Where** do you feel it in your body? *List the words that best describe this experience:*
_____
_____
_____
_____

Identify one thing you are **grateful** for today: Make sure it's different from what you identified yesterday. [Even the smallest things count] Soften your gaze/or close your eyes and take a few deep breaths as you **take a full minute** to **savor** this feeling of gratitude. *Write the details below:*
_____
_____
_____

Identify a current **need**. Go inside and ask yourself "what do I need?" *Write in third person "your name needs":*
_____
_____
_____

Starting My Day _____/_____/_____

Clear out some mental space. *Briefly describe the strongest thought or stressor that is on your mind – Label the emotion.*

_____

_____

_____

Body Location: _____ Body Sensation: _____

RVRR Part 1: Take a minute to perform part 1 of the RVRR technique. Now, set a plan for when, where and how you will release your vault later today. *Write your plan below:*

_____

_____

_____

Picture just one aspect of your ultimate dream life: Do not plan or strategize about how it's going to happen. **Just picture the final result**. Soften your gaze/or close your eyes and take a few deep breaths as you imagine and connect this part of your ultimate dream life. **Take a full minute** to **enjoy** this experience. How does this part of your ultimate dream life look and feel? *Write the words "What if...?" and then describe this specific aspect of your ultimate dream life.*

_____

_____

_____

_____

_____

Look deep into yourself: See and feel who you are at your core - your values, essence, innate abilities, and your heart. What images and qualities represent the real you? **Affirm** your unique personality. *List the words that best describe you:*

_____

_____

_____

_____

Ending My Day _____/_____/_____

List two things that went your way today. [Even the smallest things are good to notice]

1._____

2._____

RVRR Part 2: Did you release your vault? How did it go? *Write about it here:*
_____
_____
_____

Visualize a person, place, animal, or higher self that makes you feel safe and loved: **Imagine** and feel this essence. Soften your gaze/or close your eyes and take a few deep breaths as you connect. **Feel** and sense the loving, caring, and safe contact. Allow yourself to **melt** into the most soothing and comforting embrace. Allow yourself to **stay here for a full minute**. Is there a **sensation** or a **message** that comes to you? **Where** do you feel it in your body? *List the words that best describe this experience:*
_____
_____
_____
_____

Identify one thing you are **grateful** for today: Make sure it's different from what you identified yesterday. [Even the smallest things count] Soften your gaze/or close your eyes and take a few deep breaths as you **take a full minute** to **savor** this feeling of gratitude. *Write the details below:*
_____
_____
_____

Identify a current **need**. Go inside and ask yourself "what do I need?" *Write in third person "your name needs":*
_____
_____
_____

Starting My Day _____/_____/_____

Clear out some mental space. *Briefly describe the strongest thought or stressor that is on your mind – Label the emotion.*

_____

_____

_____

Body Location: _____ Body Sensation: _____

RVRR Part 1: Take a minute to perform part 1 of the RVRR technique. Now, set a plan for when, where and how you will release your vault later today. *Write your plan below:*

_____

_____

_____

Picture just one aspect of your ultimate dream life: Do not plan or strategize about how it's going to happen. **Just picture the final result**. Soften your gaze/or close your eyes and take a few deep breaths as you imagine and connect this part of your ultimate dream life. **Take a full minute** to **enjoy** this experience. How does this part of your ultimate dream life look and feel? *Write the words "What if...?" and then describe this specific aspect of your ultimate dream life.*

_____

_____

_____

_____

_____

Look deep into yourself: See and feel who you are at your core - your values, essence, innate abilities, and your heart. What images and qualities represent the real you? **Affirm** your unique personality. *List the words that best describe you:*

_____

_____

_____

_____

Ending My Day _____/_____/_____

List two things that went your way today. [Even the smallest things are good to notice]

1._____

2._____

RVRR Part 2: Did you release your vault? How did it go? *Write about it here:*

_____

_____

Visualize a person, place, animal, or higher self that makes you feel safe and loved: **Imagine** and feel this essence. Soften your gaze/or close your eyes and take a few deep breaths as you connect. **Feel** and sense the loving, caring, and safe contact. Allow yourself to **melt** into the most soothing and comforting embrace. Allow yourself to **stay here for a full minute.** Is there a **sensation** or a **message** that comes to you? **Where** do you feel it in your body? *List the words that best describe this experience:*

_____

_____

_____

Identify one thing you are **grateful** for today: Make sure it's different from what you identified yesterday. [Even the smallest things count] Soften your gaze/or close your eyes and take a few deep breaths as you **take a full minute** to **savor** this feeling of gratitude. *Write the details below:*

_____

_____

_____

Identify a current **need**. Go inside and ask yourself "what do I need?" *Write in third person "your name needs":*

_____

_____

Starting My Day _____/_____/_____

Clear out some mental space. *Briefly describe the strongest thought or stressor that is on your mind – Label the emotion.*

_____

_____

_____

Body Location: _____ Body Sensation: _____

RVRR Part 1: Take a minute to perform part 1 of the RVRR technique. Now, set a plan for when, where and how you will release your vault later today. *Write your plan below:*

_____

_____

_____

Picture just one aspect of your ultimate dream life: Do not plan or strategize about how it's going to happen. **Just picture the final result**. Soften your gaze/or close your eyes and take a few deep breaths as you imagine and connect this part of your ultimate dream life. **Take a full minute** to **enjoy** this experience. How does this part of your ultimate dream life look and feel? *Write the words "What if...?" and then describe this specific aspect of your ultimate dream life.*

_____

_____

_____

_____

_____

Look deep into yourself: See and feel who you are at your core - your values, essence, innate abilities, and your heart. What images and qualities represent the real you? **Affirm** your unique personality. *List the words that best describe you:*

_____

_____

_____

_____

Ending My Day _____/_____/_____

List two things that went your way today. [Even the smallest things are good to notice]

1._____

2._____

RVRR Part 2: Did you release your vault? How did it go? *Write about it here:*
_____
_____

Visualize a person, place, animal, or higher self that makes you feel safe and loved: **Imagine** and feel this essence. Soften your gaze/or close your eyes and take a few deep breaths as you connect. **Feel** and sense the loving, caring, and safe contact. Allow yourself to **melt** into the most soothing and comforting embrace. Allow yourself to **stay here for a full minute.** Is there a **sensation** or a **message** that comes to you? **Where** do you feel it in your body? *List the words that best describe this experience:*
_____
_____
_____

Identify one thing you are **grateful** for today: Make sure it's different from what you identified yesterday. [Even the smallest things count] Soften your gaze/or close your eyes and take a few deep breaths as you **take a full minute** to **savor** this feeling of gratitude. *Write the details below:*
_____
_____

Identify a current **need.** Go inside and ask yourself "what do I need?" *Write in third person "your name needs":*
_____
_____

Starting My Day _____/_____/_____

Clear out some mental space. *Briefly describe the strongest thought or stressor that is on your mind – Label the emotion.*

_____

_____

_____

Body Location: _____ Body Sensation: _____

RVRR Part 1: Take a minute to perform part 1 of the RVRR technique. Now, set a plan for when, where and how you will release your vault later today. *Write your plan below:*

_____

_____

_____

Picture just one aspect of your ultimate dream life: Do not plan or strategize about how it's going to happen. **Just picture the final result**. Soften your gaze/or close your eyes and take a few deep breaths as you imagine and connect this part of your ultimate dream life. **Take a full minute** to **enjoy** this experience. How does this part of your ultimate dream life look and feel? *Write the words "What if…?" and then describe this specific aspect of your ultimate dream life.*

_____

_____

_____

_____

_____

Look deep into yourself: See and feel who you are at your core - your values, essence, innate abilities, and your heart. What images and qualities represent the real you? **Affirm** your unique personality. *List the words that best describe you:*

_____

_____

_____

_____

Ending My Day _____/_____/_____

List two things that went your way today. [Even the smallest things are good to notice]

1._____

2._____

RVRR Part 2: Did you release your vault? How did it go? *Write about it here:*

_____

_____

_____

Visualize a person, place, animal, or higher self that makes you feel safe and loved: **Imagine** and feel this essence. Soften your gaze/or close your eyes and take a few deep breaths as you connect. **Feel** and sense the loving, caring, and safe contact. Allow yourself to **melt** into the most soothing and comforting embrace. Allow yourself to **stay here for a full minute**. Is there a **sensation** or a **message** that comes to you? **Where** do you feel it in your body? *List the words that best describe this experience:*

_____

_____

_____

_____

Identify one thing you are **grateful** for today: Make sure it's different from what you identified yesterday. [Even the smallest things count] Soften your gaze/or close your eyes and take a few deep breaths as you **take a full minute** to **savor** this feeling of gratitude. *Write the details below:*

_____

_____

_____

Identify a current **need**. Go inside and ask yourself "what do I need?" *Write in third person "your name needs":*

_____

_____

_____

Starting My Day _____/_____/_____

Clear out some mental space. *Briefly describe the strongest thought or stressor that is on your mind – Label the emotion.*

_____
_____
_____

Body Location: _____ Body Sensation: _____

RVRR Part 1: Take a minute to perform part 1 of the RVRR technique. Now, set a plan for when, where and how you will release your vault later today. *Write your plan below:*

_____
_____
_____

Picture just one aspect of your ultimate dream life: Do not plan or strategize about how it's going to happen. **Just picture the final result**. Soften your gaze/or close your eyes and take a few deep breaths as you imagine and connect this part of your ultimate dream life. **Take a full minute** to **enjoy** this experience. How does this part of your ultimate dream life look and feel? *Write the words "What if…?" and then describe this specific aspect of your ultimate dream life.*

_____
_____
_____
_____
_____

Look deep into yourself: See and feel who you are at your core - your values, essence, innate abilities, and your heart. What images and qualities represent the real you? **Affirm** your unique personality. *List the words that best describe you:*

_____
_____
_____
_____
_____

@QuantumMindframe

Ending My Day _____/_____/_____

List two things that went your way today. [Even the smallest things are good to notice]

1._____

2._____

RVRR Part 2: Did you release your vault? How did it go? *Write about it here:*

_____

_____

_____

Visualize a person, place, animal, or higher self that makes you feel safe and loved: **Imagine** and feel this essence. Soften your gaze/or close your eyes and take a few deep breaths as you connect. **Feel** and sense the loving, caring, and safe contact. Allow yourself to **melt** into the most soothing and comforting embrace. Allow yourself to **stay here for a full minute**. Is there a **sensation** or a **message** that comes to you? **Where** do you feel it in your body? *List the words that best describe this experience:*

_____

_____

_____

Identify one thing you are **grateful** for today: Make sure it's different from what you identified yesterday. [Even the smallest things count] Soften your gaze/or close your eyes and take a few deep breaths as you **take a full minute** to **savor** this feeling of gratitude. *Write the details below:*

_____

_____

_____

Identify a current **need**. Go inside and ask yourself "what do I need?" *Write in third person "your name needs":*

_____

_____

_____

Starting My Day _____/_____/_____

Clear out some mental space. *Briefly describe the strongest thought or stressor that is on your mind – Label the emotion.*

_____

_____

_____

Body Location: _____ Body Sensation: _____

RVRR Part 1: Take a minute to perform part 1 of the RVRR technique. Now, set a plan for when, where and how you will release your vault later today. *Write your plan below:*

_____

_____

_____

Picture just one aspect of your ultimate dream life: Do not plan or strategize about how it's going to happen. **Just picture the final result**. Soften your gaze/or close your eyes and take a few deep breaths as you imagine and connect this part of your ultimate dream life. **Take a full minute** to **enjoy** this experience. How does this part of your ultimate dream life look and feel? *Write the words "What if…?" and then describe this specific aspect of your ultimate dream life.*

_____

_____

_____

_____

_____

Look deep into yourself: See and feel who you are at your core - your values, essence, innate abilities, and your heart. What images and qualities represent the real you? **Affirm** your unique personality. *List the words that best describe you:*

_____

_____

_____

_____

_____

Ending My Day _____/_____/_____

List two things that went your way today. [Even the smallest things are good to notice]

1._____

2._____

RVRR Part 2: Did you release your vault? How did it go? *Write about it here:*

_____

_____

_____

Visualize a person, place, animal, or higher self that makes you feel safe and loved: **Imagine** and feel this essence. Soften your gaze/or close your eyes and take a few deep breaths as you connect. **Feel** and sense the loving, caring, and safe contact. Allow yourself to **melt** into the most soothing and comforting embrace. Allow yourself to **stay here for a full minute**. Is there a **sensation** or a **message** that comes to you? **Where** do you feel it in your body? *List the words that best describe this experience:*

_____

_____

_____

_____

Identify one thing you are **grateful** for today: Make sure it's different from what you identified yesterday. [Even the smallest things count] Soften your gaze/or close your eyes and take a few deep breaths as you **take a full minute** to **savor** this feeling of gratitude. *Write the details below:*

_____

_____

_____

Identify a current **need**. Go inside and ask yourself "what do I need?" *Write in third person "your name needs":*

_____

_____

_____

Starting My Day _____ / _____ / _____

Clear out some mental space. *Briefly describe the strongest thought or stressor that is on your mind – Label the emotion.*

_____

_____

Body Location: _____ Body Sensation: _____

RVRR Part 1: Take a minute to perform part 1 of the RVRR technique. Now, set a plan for when, where and how you will release your vault later today. *Write your plan below:*

_____

_____

_____

Picture just one aspect of your ultimate dream life: Do not plan or strategize about how it's going to happen. **Just picture the final result**. Soften your gaze/or close your eyes and take a few deep breaths as you imagine and connect this part of your ultimate dream life. **Take a full minute** to **enjoy** this experience. How does this part of your ultimate dream life look and feel? *Write the words "What if...?" and then describe this specific aspect of your ultimate dream life.*

_____

_____

_____

_____

_____

Look deep into yourself: See and feel who you are at your core - your values, essence, innate abilities, and your heart. What images and qualities represent the real you? **Affirm** your unique personality. *List the words that best describe you:*

_____

_____

_____

_____

Ending My Day _____/_____/_____

List two things that went your way today. [Even the smallest things are good to notice]

1._____
2._____

RVRR Part 2: Did you release your vault? How did it go? *Write about it here:*
_____
_____
_____

Visualize a person, place, animal, or higher self that makes you feel safe and loved: **Imagine** and feel this essence. Soften your gaze/or close your eyes and take a few deep breaths as you connect. **Feel** and sense the loving, caring, and safe contact. Allow yourself to **melt** into the most soothing and comforting embrace. Allow yourself to **stay here for a full minute.** Is there a **sensation** or a **message** that comes to you? **Where** do you feel it in your body? *List the words that best describe this experience:*
_____
_____
_____
_____

Identify one thing you are **grateful** for today: Make sure it's different from what you identified yesterday. [Even the smallest things count] Soften your gaze/or close your eyes and take a few deep breaths as you **take a full minute** to **savor** this feeling of gratitude. *Write the details below:*
_____
_____
_____

Identify a current **need**. Go inside and ask yourself "what do I need?" *Write in third person "your name needs":*
_____
_____
_____

Starting My Day _____/_____/_____

Clear out some mental space. *Briefly describe the strongest thought or stressor that is on your mind – Label the emotion.*

_____
_____
_____

Body Location: _____ Body Sensation: _____

RVRR Part 1: Take a minute to perform part 1 of the RVRR technique. Now, set a plan for when, where and how you will release your vault later today. *Write your plan below:*

_____
_____
_____

Picture just one aspect of your ultimate dream life: Do not plan or strategize about how it's going to happen. **Just picture the final result**. Soften your gaze/or close your eyes and take a few deep breaths as you imagine and connect this part of your ultimate dream life. **Take a full minute** to **enjoy** this experience. How does this part of your ultimate dream life look and feel? *Write the words "What if...?" and then describe this specific aspect of your ultimate dream life.*

_____
_____
_____
_____
_____

Look deep into yourself: See and feel who you are at your core - your values, essence, innate abilities, and your heart. What images and qualities represent the real you? **Affirm** your unique personality. *List the words that best describe you:*

_____
_____
_____
_____

Ending My Day _____/_____/_____

List two things that went your way today. [Even the smallest things are good to notice]

1._____

2._____

RVRR Part 2: Did you release your vault? How did it go? *Write about it here:*
_____
_____

Visualize a person, place, animal, or higher self that makes you feel safe and loved: **Imagine** and feel this essence. Soften your gaze/or close your eyes and take a few deep breaths as you connect. **Feel** and sense the loving, caring, and safe contact. Allow yourself to **melt** into the most soothing and comforting embrace. Allow yourself to **stay here for a full minute.** Is there a **sensation** or a **message** that comes to you? **Where** do you feel it in your body? *List the words that best describe this experience:*
_____
_____
_____

Identify one thing you are **grateful** for today: Make sure it's different from what you identified yesterday. [Even the smallest things count] Soften your gaze/or close your eyes and take a few deep breaths as you **take a full minute** to **savor** this feeling of gratitude. *Write the details below:*
_____
_____
_____

Identify a current **need**. Go inside and ask yourself "what do I need?" *Write in third person "your name needs":*
_____
_____
_____

Starting My Day _____/_____/_____

Clear out some mental space. *Briefly describe the strongest thought or stressor that is on your mind – Label the emotion.*

_____

_____

_____

Body Location: _____ Body Sensation: _____

RVRR Part 1: Take a minute to perform part 1 of the RVRR technique. Now, set a plan for when, where and how you will release your vault later today. *Write your plan below:*

_____

_____

_____

Picture just one aspect of your ultimate dream life: Do not plan or strategize about how it's going to happen. **Just picture the final result**. Soften your gaze/or close your eyes and take a few deep breaths as you imagine and connect this part of your ultimate dream life. **Take a full minute** to **enjoy** this experience. How does this part of your ultimate dream life look and feel? *Write the words "What if...?" and then describe this specific aspect of your ultimate dream life.*

_____

_____

_____

_____

_____

Look deep into yourself: See and feel who you are at your core - your values, essence, innate abilities, and your heart. What images and qualities represent the real you? **Affirm** your unique personality. *List the words that best describe you:*

_____

_____

_____

_____

Ending My Day _____/_____/_____

List two things that went your way today. [Even the smallest things are good to notice]

1._____

2._____

RVRR Part 2: Did you release your vault? How did it go? *Write about it here:*

_____

_____

_____

Visualize a person, place, animal, or higher self that makes you feel safe and loved: **Imagine** and feel this essence. Soften your gaze/or close your eyes and take a few deep breaths as you connect. **Feel** and sense the loving, caring, and safe contact. Allow yourself to **melt** into the most soothing and comforting embrace. Allow yourself to **stay here for a full minute**. Is there a **sensation** or a **message** that comes to you? **Where** do you feel it in your body? *List the words that best describe this experience:*

_____

_____

_____

_____

Identify one thing you are **grateful** for today: Make sure it's different from what you identified yesterday. [Even the smallest things count] Soften your gaze/or close your eyes and take a few deep breaths as you **take a full minute** to **savor** this feeling of gratitude. *Write the details below:*

_____

_____

_____

Identify a current **need**. Go inside and ask yourself "what do I need?" *Write in third person "your name needs":*

_____

_____

_____

Starting My Day _____/_____/_____

Clear out some mental space. *Briefly describe the strongest thought or stressor that is on your mind – Label the emotion.*

_____

_____

_____

Body Location: _____ Body Sensation: _____

RVRR Part 1: Take a minute to perform part 1 of the RVRR technique. Now, set a plan for when, where and how you will release your vault later today. *Write your plan below:*

_____

_____

_____

Picture just one aspect of your ultimate dream life: Do not plan or strategize about how it's going to happen. **Just picture the final result**. Soften your gaze/or close your eyes and take a few deep breaths as you imagine and connect this part of your ultimate dream life. **Take a full minute** to **enjoy** this experience. How does this part of your ultimate dream life look and feel? *Write the words "What if…?" and then describe this specific aspect of your ultimate dream life.*

_____

_____

_____

_____

_____

Look deep into yourself: See and feel who you are at your core - your values, essence, innate abilities, and your heart. What images and qualities represent the real you? **Affirm** your unique personality. *List the words that best describe you:*

_____

_____

_____

_____

Ending My Day _____/_____/_____

List two things that went your way today. [Even the smallest things are good to notice]

1._____

2._____

RVRR Part 2: Did you release your vault? How did it go? *Write about it here:*

_____

_____

_____

Visualize a person, place, animal, or higher self that makes you feel safe and loved: **Imagine** and feel this essence. Soften your gaze/or close your eyes and take a few deep breaths as you connect. **Feel** and sense the loving, caring, and safe contact. Allow yourself to **melt** into the most soothing and comforting embrace. Allow yourself to **stay here for a full minute**. Is there a **sensation** or a **message** that comes to you? **Where** do you feel it in your body? *List the words that best describe this experience:*

_____

_____

_____

_____

Identify one thing you are **grateful** for today: Make sure it's different from what you identified yesterday. [Even the smallest things count] Soften your gaze/or close your eyes and take a few deep breaths as you **take a full minute** to **savor** this feeling of gratitude. *Write the details below:*

_____

_____

_____

Identify a current **need**. Go inside and ask yourself "what do I need?" *Write in third person "your name needs":*

_____

_____

_____

Starting My Day _____/_____/_____

Clear out some mental space. *Briefly describe the strongest thought or stressor that is on your mind – Label the emotion.*

_____

_____

_____

Body Location: _____ Body Sensation: _____

RVRR Part 1: Take a minute to perform part 1 of the RVRR technique. Now, set a plan for when, where and how you will release your vault later today. *Write your plan below:*

_____

_____

_____

Picture just one aspect of your ultimate dream life: Do not plan or strategize about how it's going to happen. **Just picture the final result.** Soften your gaze/or close your eyes and take a few deep breaths as you imagine and connect this part of your ultimate dream life. **Take a full minute** to **enjoy** this experience. How does this part of your ultimate dream life look and feel? *Write the words "What if…?" and then describe this specific aspect of your ultimate dream life.*

_____

_____

_____

_____

_____

Look deep into yourself: See and feel who you are at your core - your values, essence, innate abilities, and your heart. What images and qualities represent the real you? **Affirm** your unique personality. *List the words that best describe you:*

_____

_____

_____

_____

Ending My Day _____/_____/_____

List two things that went your way today. [Even the smallest things are good to notice]

1._____

2._____

RVRR Part 2: Did you release your vault? How did it go? *Write about it here:*
_____
_____
_____

Visualize a person, place, animal, or higher self that makes you feel safe and loved: **Imagine** and feel this essence. Soften your gaze/or close your eyes and take a few deep breaths as you connect. **Feel** and sense the loving, caring, and safe contact. Allow yourself to **melt** into the most soothing and comforting embrace. Allow yourself to **stay here for a full minute**. Is there a **sensation** or a **message** that comes to you? **Where** do you feel it in your body? *List the words that best describe this experience:*
_____
_____
_____
_____

Identify one thing you are **grateful** for today: Make sure it's different from what you identified yesterday. [Even the smallest things count] Soften your gaze/or close your eyes and take a few deep breaths as you **take a full minute** to **savor** this feeling of gratitude. *Write the details below:*
_____
_____
_____

Identify a current **need**. Go inside and ask yourself "what do I need?" *Write in third person "your name needs":*
_____
_____
_____

Starting My Day _____/_____/_____

Clear out some mental space. *Briefly describe the strongest thought or stressor that is on your mind – Label the emotion.*

_____

_____

_____

Body Location: _____ Body Sensation: _____

RVRR Part 1: Take a minute to perform part 1 of the RVRR technique. Now, set a plan for when, where and how you will release your vault later today. *Write your plan below:*

_____

_____

_____

Picture just one aspect of your ultimate dream life: Do not plan or strategize about how it's going to happen. **Just picture the final result**. Soften your gaze/or close your eyes and take a few deep breaths as you imagine and connect this part of your ultimate dream life. **Take a full minute** to **enjoy** this experience. How does this part of your ultimate dream life look and feel? *Write the words "What if...?" and then describe this specific aspect of your ultimate dream life.*

_____

_____

_____

_____

_____

Look deep into yourself: See and feel who you are at your core - your values, essence, innate abilities, and your heart. What images and qualities represent the real you? **Affirm** your unique personality. *List the words that best describe you:*

_____

_____

_____

_____

@QuantumMindframe

Ending My Day _____/_____/_____

List two things that went your way today. [Even the smallest things are good to notice]

1._____

2._____

RVRR Part 2: Did you release your vault? How did it go? *Write about it here:*
_____
_____

Visualize a person, place, animal, or higher self that makes you feel safe and loved: **Imagine** and feel this essence. Soften your gaze/or close your eyes and take a few deep breaths as you connect. **Feel** and sense the loving, caring, and safe contact. Allow yourself to **melt** into the most soothing and comforting embrace. Allow yourself to **stay here for a full minute.** Is there a **sensation** or a **message** that comes to you? **Where** do you feel it in your body? *List the words that best describe this experience:*
_____
_____
_____

Identify one thing you are **grateful** for today: Make sure it's different from what you identified yesterday. [Even the smallest things count] Soften your gaze/or close your eyes and take a few deep breaths as you **take a full minute** to **savor** this feeling of gratitude. *Write the details below:*
_____
_____
_____

Identify a current **need**. Go inside and ask yourself "what do I need?" *Write in third person "your name needs":*
_____
_____
_____

Starting My Day _____/_____/_____

Clear out some mental space. *Briefly describe the strongest thought or stressor that is on your mind – Label the emotion.*

_____

_____

_____

Body Location: _____ Body Sensation: _____

RVRR Part 1: Take a minute to perform part 1 of the RVRR technique. Now, set a plan for when, where and how you will release your vault later today. *Write your plan below:*

_____

_____

_____

Picture just one aspect of your ultimate dream life: Do not plan or strategize about how it's going to happen. **Just picture the final result.** Soften your gaze/or close your eyes and take a few deep breaths as you imagine and connect this part of your ultimate dream life. **Take a full minute** to **enjoy** this experience. How does this part of your ultimate dream life look and feel? *Write the words "What if...?" and then describe this specific aspect of your ultimate dream life.*

_____

_____

_____

_____

_____

Look deep into yourself: See and feel who you are at your core - your values, essence, innate abilities, and your heart. What images and qualities represent the real you? **Affirm** your unique personality. *List the words that best describe you:*

_____

_____

_____

_____

_____

Ending My Day _____/_____/_____

List two things that went your way today. [Even the smallest things are good to notice]

1._____
2._____

RVRR Part 2: Did you release your vault? How did it go? *Write about it here:*
_____
_____
_____

Visualize a person, place, animal, or higher self that makes you feel safe and loved: **Imagine** and feel this essence. Soften your gaze/or close your eyes and take a few deep breaths as you connect. **Feel** and sense the loving, caring, and safe contact. Allow yourself to **melt** into the most soothing and comforting embrace. Allow yourself to **stay here for a full minute.** Is there a **sensation** or a **message** that comes to you? **Where** do you feel it in your body? *List the words that best describe this experience:*
_____
_____
_____
_____

Identify one thing you are **grateful** for today: Make sure it's different from what you identified yesterday. [Even the smallest things count] Soften your gaze/or close your eyes and take a few deep breaths as you **take a full minute** to **savor** this feeling of gratitude. *Write the details below:*
_____
_____
_____

Identify a current **need**. Go inside and ask yourself "what do I need?" *Write in third person "your name needs":*
_____
_____
_____

Starting My Day _____/_____/_____

Clear out some mental space. *Briefly describe the strongest thought or stressor that is on your mind – Label the emotion.*

_____

_____

_____

Body Location: _____ Body Sensation: _____

RVRR Part 1: Take a minute to perform part 1 of the RVRR technique. Now, set a plan for when, where and how you will release your vault later today. *Write your plan below:*

_____

_____

_____

Picture just one aspect of your ultimate dream life: Do not plan or strategize about how it's going to happen. **Just picture the final result**. Soften your gaze/or close your eyes and take a few deep breaths as you imagine and connect this part of your ultimate dream life. **Take a full minute** to **enjoy** this experience. How does this part of your ultimate dream life look and feel? *Write the words "What if...?" and then describe this specific aspect of your ultimate dream life.*

_____

_____

_____

_____

_____

Look deep into yourself: See and feel who you are at your core - your values, essence, innate abilities, and your heart. What images and qualities represent the real you? **Affirm** your unique personality. *List the words that best describe you:*

_____

_____

_____

_____

@QuantumMindframe

Ending My Day _____/_____/_____

List two things that went your way today. [Even the smallest things are good to notice]

1._____

2._____

RVRR Part 2: Did you release your vault? How did it go? *Write about it here:*
_____
_____

Visualize a person, place, animal, or higher self that makes you feel safe and loved: **Imagine** and feel this essence. Soften your gaze/or close your eyes and take a few deep breaths as you connect. **Feel** and sense the loving, caring, and safe contact. Allow yourself to **melt** into the most soothing and comforting embrace. Allow yourself to **stay here for a full minute.** Is there a **sensation** or a **message** that comes to you? **Where** do you feel it in your body? *List the words that best describe this experience:*
_____
_____
_____

Identify one thing you are **grateful** for today: Make sure it's different from what you identified yesterday. [Even the smallest things count] Soften your gaze/or close your eyes and take a few deep breaths as you **take a full minute** to **savor** this feeling of gratitude. *Write the details below:*
_____
_____
_____

Identify a current **need**. Go inside and ask yourself "what do I need?" *Write in third person "your name needs":*
_____
_____
_____

Starting My Day _____/_____/_____

Clear out some mental space. *Briefly describe the strongest thought or stressor that is on your mind – Label the emotion.*

_____

_____

_____

Body Location: _____ Body Sensation: _____

RVRR Part 1: Take a minute to perform part 1 of the RVRR technique. Now, set a plan for when, where and how you will release your vault later today. *Write your plan below:*

_____

_____

_____

Picture just one aspect of your ultimate dream life: Do not plan or strategize about how it's going to happen. **Just picture the final result**. Soften your gaze/or close your eyes and take a few deep breaths as you imagine and connect this part of your ultimate dream life. **Take a full minute** to **enjoy** this experience. How does this part of your ultimate dream life look and feel? *Write the words "What if…?" and then describe this specific aspect of your ultimate dream life.*

_____

_____

_____

_____

_____

Look deep into yourself: See and feel who you are at your core - your values, essence, innate abilities, and your heart. What images and qualities represent the real you? **Affirm** your unique personality. *List the words that best describe you:*

_____

_____

_____

_____

Ending My Day _____/_____/_____

List two things that went your way today. [Even the smallest things are good to notice]

1._____

2._____

RVRR Part 2: Did you release your vault? How did it go? *Write about it here:*

_____
_____
_____

Visualize a person, place, animal, or higher self that makes you feel safe and loved: **Imagine** and feel this essence. Soften your gaze/or close your eyes and take a few deep breaths as you connect. **Feel** and sense the loving, caring, and safe contact. Allow yourself to **melt** into the most soothing and comforting embrace. Allow yourself to **stay here for a full minute**. Is there a **sensation** or a **message** that comes to you? **Where** do you feel it in your body? *List the words that best describe this experience:*

_____
_____
_____

Identify one thing you are **grateful** for today: Make sure it's different from what you identified yesterday. [Even the smallest things count] Soften your gaze/or close your eyes and take a few deep breaths as you **take a full minute** to **savor** this feeling of gratitude. *Write the details below:*

_____
_____

Identify a current **need**. Go inside and ask yourself "what do I need?" *Write in third person "your name needs":*

_____
_____

Starting My Day _____/_____/_____

Clear out some mental space. *Briefly describe the strongest thought or stressor that is on your mind – Label the emotion.*

_____

_____

_____

Body Location: _____ Body Sensation: _____

RVRR Part 1: Take a minute to perform part 1 of the RVRR technique. Now, set a plan for when, where and how you will release your vault later today. *Write your plan below:*

_____

_____

_____

Picture just one aspect of your ultimate dream life: Do not plan or strategize about how it's going to happen. **Just picture the final result**. Soften your gaze/or close your eyes and take a few deep breaths as you imagine and connect this part of your ultimate dream life. **Take a full minute** to **enjoy** this experience. How does this part of your ultimate dream life look and feel? *Write the words "What if…?" and then describe this specific aspect of your ultimate dream life.*

_____

_____

_____

_____

_____

Look deep into yourself: See and feel who you are at your core - your values, essence, innate abilities, and your heart. What images and qualities represent the real you? **Affirm** your unique personality. *List the words that best describe you:*

_____

_____

_____

_____

Ending My Day _____/_____/_____

List two things that went your way today. [Even the smallest things are good to notice]

1._____

2._____

RVRR Part 2: Did you release your vault? How did it go? *Write about it here:*

_____
_____
_____

Visualize a person, place, animal, or higher self that makes you feel safe and loved: **Imagine** and feel this essence. Soften your gaze/or close your eyes and take a few deep breaths as you connect. **Feel** and sense the loving, caring, and safe contact. Allow yourself to **melt** into the most soothing and comforting embrace. Allow yourself to **stay here for a full minute.** Is there a **sensation** or a **message** that comes to you? **Where** do you feel it in your body? *List the words that best describe this experience:*

_____
_____
_____
_____

Identify one thing you are **grateful** for today: Make sure it's different from what you identified yesterday. [Even the smallest things count] Soften your gaze/or close your eyes and take a few deep breaths as you **take a full minute** to **savor** this feeling of gratitude. *Write the details below:*

_____
_____
_____

Identify a current **need**. Go inside and ask yourself "what do I need?" *Write in third person "your name needs":*

_____
_____
_____

Starting My Day _____/_____/_____

Clear out some mental space. *Briefly describe the strongest thought or stressor that is on your mind – Label the emotion.*

_____

_____

_____

Body Location: _____ Body Sensation: _____

RVRR Part 1: Take a minute to perform part 1 of the RVRR technique. Now, set a plan for when, where and how you will release your vault later today. *Write your plan below:*

_____

_____

_____

Picture just one aspect of your ultimate dream life: Do not plan or strategize about how it's going to happen. **Just picture the final result**. Soften your gaze/or close your eyes and take a few deep breaths as you imagine and connect this part of your ultimate dream life. **Take a full minute** to **enjoy** this experience. How does this part of your ultimate dream life look and feel? *Write the words "What if…?" and then describe this specific aspect of your ultimate dream life.*

_____

_____

_____

_____

_____

Look deep into yourself: See and feel who you are at your core - your values, essence, innate abilities, and your heart. What images and qualities represent the real you? **Affirm** your unique personality. *List the words that best describe you:*

_____

_____

_____

_____

Ending My Day _____/_____/_____

List two things that went your way today. [Even the smallest things are good to notice]

1._____

2._____

RVRR Part 2: Did you release your vault? How did it go? *Write about it here:*

_____

_____

_____

Visualize a person, place, animal, or higher self that makes you feel safe and loved: **Imagine** and feel this essence. Soften your gaze/or close your eyes and take a few deep breaths as you connect. **Feel** and sense the loving, caring, and safe contact. Allow yourself to **melt** into the most soothing and comforting embrace. Allow yourself to **stay here for a full minute**. Is there a **sensation** or a **message** that comes to you? **Where** do you feel it in your body? *List the words that best describe this experience:*

_____

_____

_____

_____

Identify one thing you are **grateful** for today: Make sure it's different from what you identified yesterday. [Even the smallest things count] Soften your gaze/or close your eyes and take a few deep breaths as you **take a full minute** to **savor** this feeling of gratitude. *Write the details below:*

_____

_____

_____

Identify a current **need**. Go inside and ask yourself "what do I need?" *Write in third person "your name needs":*

_____

_____

_____

Starting My Day _____/_____/_____

Clear out some mental space. *Briefly describe the strongest thought or stressor that is on your mind – Label the emotion.*

_____

_____

_____

Body Location: _____ Body Sensation: _____

RVRR Part 1: Take a minute to perform part 1 of the RVRR technique. Now, set a plan for when, where and how you will release your vault later today. *Write your plan below:*

_____

_____

_____

Picture just one aspect of your ultimate dream life: Do not plan or strategize about how it's going to happen. **Just picture the final result.** Soften your gaze/or close your eyes and take a few deep breaths as you imagine and connect this part of your ultimate dream life. **Take a full minute** to **enjoy** this experience. How does this part of your ultimate dream life look and feel? *Write the words "What if...?" and then describe this specific aspect of your ultimate dream life.*

_____

_____

_____

_____

_____

Look deep into yourself: See and feel who you are at your core - your values, essence, innate abilities, and your heart. What images and qualities represent the real you? **Affirm** your unique personality. *List the words that best describe you:*

_____

_____

_____

_____

Ending My Day _____/_____/_____

List two things that went your way today. [Even the smallest things are good to notice]

1._____

2._____

RVRR Part 2: Did you release your vault? How did it go? *Write about it here:*

_____

_____

_____

Visualize a person, place, animal, or higher self that makes you feel safe and loved: **Imagine** and feel this essence. Soften your gaze/or close your eyes and take a few deep breaths as you connect. **Feel** and sense the loving, caring, and safe contact. Allow yourself to **melt** into the most soothing and comforting embrace. Allow yourself to **stay here for a full minute**. Is there a **sensation** or a **message** that comes to you? **Where** do you feel it in your body? *List the words that best describe this experience:*

_____

_____

_____

_____

Identify one thing you are **grateful** for today: Make sure it's different from what you identified yesterday. [Even the smallest things count] Soften your gaze/or close your eyes and take a few deep breaths as you **take a full minute** to **savor** this feeling of gratitude. *Write the details below:*

_____

_____

_____

Identify a current **need**. Go inside and ask yourself "what do I need?" *Write in third person "your name needs":*

_____

_____

_____

Starting My Day _____/_____/_____

Clear out some mental space. *Briefly describe the strongest thought or stressor that is on your mind – Label the emotion.*

_____

_____

_____

Body Location: _____ Body Sensation: _____

RVRR Part 1: Take a minute to perform part 1 of the RVRR technique. Now, set a plan for when, where and how you will release your vault later today. *Write your plan below:*

_____

_____

_____

Picture just one aspect of your ultimate dream life: Do not plan or strategize about how it's going to happen. **Just picture the final result**. Soften your gaze/or close your eyes and take a few deep breaths as you imagine and connect this part of your ultimate dream life. **Take a full minute** to **enjoy** this experience. How does this part of your ultimate dream life look and feel? *Write the words "What if…?" and then describe this specific aspect of your ultimate dream life.*

_____

_____

_____

_____

_____

Look deep into yourself: See and feel who you are at your core - your values, essence, innate abilities, and your heart. What images and qualities represent the real you? **Affirm** your unique personality. *List the words that best describe you:*

_____

_____

_____

_____

Ending My Day _____/_____/_____

List two things that went your way today. [Even the smallest things are good to notice]

1._____

2._____

RVRR Part 2: Did you release your vault? How did it go? *Write about it here:*

_____
_____
_____

Visualize a person, place, animal, or higher self that makes you feel safe and loved: **Imagine** and feel this essence. Soften your gaze/or close your eyes and take a few deep breaths as you connect. **Feel** and sense the loving, caring, and safe contact. Allow yourself to **melt** into the most soothing and comforting embrace. Allow yourself to **stay here for a full minute.** Is there a **sensation** or a **message** that comes to you? **Where** do you feel it in your body? *List the words that best describe this experience:*

_____
_____
_____

Identify one thing you are **grateful** for today: Make sure it's different from what you identified yesterday. [Even the smallest things count] Soften your gaze/or close your eyes and take a few deep breaths as you **take a full minute** to **savor** this feeling of gratitude. *Write the details below:*

_____
_____
_____

Identify a current **need**. Go inside and ask yourself "what do I need?" *Write in third person "your name needs":*

_____
_____
_____

Starting My Day _____/_____/_____

Clear out some mental space. *Briefly describe the strongest thought or stressor that is on your mind – Label the emotion.*

_____

_____

_____

Body Location: _____ Body Sensation: _____

RVRR Part 1: Take a minute to perform part 1 of the RVRR technique. Now, set a plan for when, where and how you will release your vault later today. *Write your plan below:*

_____

_____

_____

Picture just one aspect of your ultimate dream life: Do not plan or strategize about how it's going to happen. **Just picture the final result**. Soften your gaze/or close your eyes and take a few deep breaths as you imagine and connect this part of your ultimate dream life. **Take a full minute** to **enjoy** this experience. How does this part of your ultimate dream life look and feel? *Write the words "What if…?" and then describe this specific aspect of your ultimate dream life.*

_____

_____

_____

_____

_____

Look deep into yourself: See and feel who you are at your core - your values, essence, innate abilities, and your heart. What images and qualities represent the real you? **Affirm** your unique personality. *List the words that best describe you:*

_____

_____

_____

_____

Ending My Day _____/_____/_____

List two things that went your way today. [Even the smallest things are good to notice]

1._____

2._____

RVRR Part 2: Did you release your vault? How did it go? *Write about it here:*

_____

_____

_____

Visualize a person, place, animal, or higher self that makes you feel safe and loved: **Imagine** and feel this essence. Soften your gaze/or close your eyes and take a few deep breaths as you connect. **Feel** and sense the loving, caring, and safe contact. Allow yourself to **melt** into the most soothing and comforting embrace. Allow yourself to **stay here for a full minute.** Is there a **sensation** or a **message** that comes to you? **Where** do you feel it in your body? *List the words that best describe this experience:*

_____

_____

_____

_____

Identify one thing you are **grateful** for today: Make sure it's different from what you identified yesterday. [Even the smallest things count] Soften your gaze/or close your eyes and take a few deep breaths as you **take a full minute** to **savor** this feeling of gratitude. *Write the details below:*

_____

_____

_____

Identify a current **need**. Go inside and ask yourself "what do I need?" *Write in third person "your name needs":*

_____

_____

_____

Starting My Day _____ / _____ / _____

Clear out some mental space. *Briefly describe the strongest thought or stressor that is on your mind – Label the emotion.*

_____

_____

_____

Body Location: _____ Body Sensation: _____

RVRR Part 1: Take a minute to perform part 1 of the RVRR technique. Now, set a plan for when, where and how you will release your vault later today. *Write your plan below:*

_____

_____

_____

Picture just one aspect of your ultimate dream life: Do not plan or strategize about how it's going to happen. **Just picture the final result**. Soften your gaze/or close your eyes and take a few deep breaths as you imagine and connect this part of your ultimate dream life. **Take a full minute** to **enjoy** this experience. How does this part of your ultimate dream life look and feel? *Write the words "What if…?" and then describe this specific aspect of your ultimate dream life.*

_____

_____

_____

_____

_____

Look deep into yourself: See and feel who you are at your core - your values, essence, innate abilities, and your heart. What images and qualities represent the real you? **Affirm** your unique personality. *List the words that best describe you:*

_____

_____

_____

_____

@QuantumMindframe

Ending My Day _____/_____/_____

List two things that went your way today. [Even the smallest things are good to notice]

1._____

2._____

RVRR Part 2: Did you release your vault? How did it go? *Write about it here:*
_____
_____
_____

Visualize a person, place, animal, or higher self that makes you feel safe and loved: **Imagine** and feel this essence. Soften your gaze/or close your eyes and take a few deep breaths as you connect. **Feel** and sense the loving, caring, and safe contact. Allow yourself to **melt** into the most soothing and comforting embrace. Allow yourself to **stay here for a full minute**. Is there a **sensation** or a **message** that comes to you? **Where** do you feel it in your body? *List the words that best describe this experience:*
_____
_____
_____
_____

Identify one thing you are **grateful** for today: Make sure it's different from what you identified yesterday. [Even the smallest things count] Soften your gaze/or close your eyes and take a few deep breaths as you **take a full minute** to **savor** this feeling of gratitude. *Write the details below:*
_____
_____
_____

Identify a current **need**. Go inside and ask yourself "what do I need?" *Write in third person "your name needs":*
_____
_____
_____

Starting My Day _____/_____/_____

Clear out some mental space. *Briefly describe the strongest thought or stressor that is on your mind – Label the emotion.*

_____

_____

_____

Body Location: _____ Body Sensation: _____

RVRR Part 1: Take a minute to perform part 1 of the RVRR technique. Now, set a plan for when, where and how you will release your vault later today. *Write your plan below:*

_____

_____

_____

Picture just one aspect of your ultimate dream life: Do not plan or strategize about how it's going to happen. **Just picture the final result**. Soften your gaze/or close your eyes and take a few deep breaths as you imagine and connect this part of your ultimate dream life. **Take a full minute** to **enjoy** this experience. How does this part of your ultimate dream life look and feel? *Write the words "What if...?" and then describe this specific aspect of your ultimate dream life.*

_____

_____

_____

_____

_____

Look deep into yourself: See and feel who you are at your core - your values, essence, innate abilities, and your heart. What images and qualities represent the real you? **Affirm** your unique personality. *List the words that best describe you:*

_____

_____

_____

_____

Ending My Day _____/_____/_____

List two things that went your way today. [Even the smallest things are good to notice]

1._____

2._____

RVRR Part 2: Did you release your vault? How did it go? *Write about it here:*
_____
_____
_____

Visualize a person, place, animal, or higher self that makes you feel safe and loved: **Imagine** and feel this essence. Soften your gaze/or close your eyes and take a few deep breaths as you connect. **Feel** and sense the loving, caring, and safe contact. Allow yourself to **melt** into the most soothing and comforting embrace. Allow yourself to **stay here for a full minute**. Is there a **sensation** or a **message** that comes to you? **Where** do you feel it in your body? *List the words that best describe this experience:*
_____
_____
_____
_____

Identify one thing you are **grateful** for today: Make sure it's different from what you identified yesterday. [Even the smallest things count] Soften your gaze/or close your eyes and take a few deep breaths as you **take a full minute** to **savor** this feeling of gratitude. *Write the details below:*
_____
_____
_____

Identify a current **need**. Go inside and ask yourself "what do I need?" *Write in third person "your name needs":*
_____
_____
_____

Starting My Day _____/_____/_____

Clear out some mental space. *Briefly describe the strongest thought or stressor that is on your mind – Label the emotion.*

_____

_____

_____

Body Location: _____ Body Sensation: _____

RVRR Part 1: Take a minute to perform part 1 of the RVRR technique. Now, set a plan for when, where and how you will release your vault later today. *Write your plan below:*

_____

_____

_____

Picture just one aspect of your ultimate dream life: Do not plan or strategize about how it's going to happen. **Just picture the final result.** Soften your gaze/or close your eyes and take a few deep breaths as you imagine and connect this part of your ultimate dream life. **Take a full minute** to **enjoy** this experience. How does this part of your ultimate dream life look and feel? *Write the words "What if…?" and then describe this specific aspect of your ultimate dream life.*

_____

_____

_____

_____

_____

Look deep into yourself: See and feel who you are at your core - your values, essence, innate abilities, and your heart. What images and qualities represent the real you? **Affirm** your unique personality. *List the words that best describe you:*

_____

_____

_____

_____

Ending My Day _____/_____/_____

List two things that went your way today. [Even the smallest things are good to notice]

1._____

2._____

RVRR Part 2: Did you release your vault? How did it go? *Write about it here:*

_____

_____

Visualize a person, place, animal, or higher self that makes you feel safe and loved: **Imagine** and feel this essence. Soften your gaze/or close your eyes and take a few deep breaths as you connect. **Feel** and sense the loving, caring, and safe contact. Allow yourself to **melt** into the most soothing and comforting embrace. Allow yourself to **stay here for a full minute**. Is there a **sensation** or a **message** that comes to you? **Where** do you feel it in your body? *List the words that best describe this experience:*

_____

_____

_____

Identify one thing you are **grateful** for today: Make sure it's different from what you identified yesterday. [Even the smallest things count] Soften your gaze/or close your eyes and take a few deep breaths as you **take a full minute** to **savor** this feeling of gratitude. *Write the details below:*

_____

_____

_____

Identify a current **need**. Go inside and ask yourself "what do I need?" *Write in third person "your name needs":*

_____

_____

_____

Starting My Day _____/_____/_____

Clear out some mental space. *Briefly describe the strongest thought or stressor that is on your mind – Label the emotion.*

_____

_____

Body Location: _____ Body Sensation: _____

RVRR Part 1: Take a minute to perform part 1 of the RVRR technique. Now, set a plan for when, where and how you will release your vault later today. *Write your plan below:*

_____

_____

_____

Picture just one aspect of your ultimate dream life: Do not plan or strategize about how it's going to happen. **Just picture the final result**. Soften your gaze/or close your eyes and take a few deep breaths as you imagine and connect this part of your ultimate dream life. **Take a full minute** to **enjoy** this experience. How does this part of your ultimate dream life look and feel? *Write the words "What if...?" and then describe this specific aspect of your ultimate dream life.*

_____

_____

_____

_____

_____

Look deep into yourself: See and feel who you are at your core - your values, essence, innate abilities, and your heart. What images and qualities represent the real you? **Affirm** your unique personality. *List the words that best describe you:*

_____

_____

_____

_____

Ending My Day _____/_____/_____

List two things that went your way today. [Even the smallest things are good to notice]

1._____

2._____

RVRR Part 2: Did you release your vault? How did it go? *Write about it here:*
_____
_____
_____

Visualize a person, place, animal, or higher self that makes you feel safe and loved: **Imagine** and feel this essence. Soften your gaze/or close your eyes and take a few deep breaths as you connect. **Feel** and sense the loving, caring, and safe contact. Allow yourself to **melt** into the most soothing and comforting embrace. Allow yourself to **stay here for a full minute**. Is there a **sensation** or a **message** that comes to you? **Where** do you feel it in your body? *List the words that best describe this experience:*
_____
_____
_____
_____

Identify one thing you are **grateful** for today: Make sure it's different from what you identified yesterday. [Even the smallest things count] Soften your gaze/or close your eyes and take a few deep breaths as you **take a full minute** to **savor** this feeling of gratitude. *Write the details below:*
_____
_____
_____

Identify a current **need**. Go inside and ask yourself "what do I need?" *Write in third person "your name needs":*
_____
_____
_____

Starting My Day _____/_____/_____

Clear out some mental space. *Briefly describe the strongest thought or stressor that is on your mind – Label the emotion.*

_____

_____

_____

Body Location: _____ Body Sensation: _____

RVRR Part 1: Take a minute to perform part 1 of the RVRR technique. Now, set a plan for when, where and how you will release your vault later today. *Write your plan below:*

_____

_____

_____

Picture just one aspect of your ultimate dream life: Do not plan or strategize about how it's going to happen. **Just picture the final result.** Soften your gaze/or close your eyes and take a few deep breaths as you imagine and connect this part of your ultimate dream life. **Take a full minute** to **enjoy** this experience. How does this part of your ultimate dream life look and feel? *Write the words "What if...?" and then describe this specific aspect of your ultimate dream life.*

_____

_____

_____

_____

_____

Look deep into yourself: See and feel who you are at your core - your values, essence, innate abilities, and your heart. What images and qualities represent the real you? **Affirm** your unique personality. *List the words that best describe you:*

_____

_____

_____

_____

Ending My Day _____/_____/_____

List two things that went your way today. [Even the smallest things are good to notice]

1._____
2._____

RVRR Part 2: Did you release your vault? How did it go? *Write about it here:*
_____
_____
_____

Visualize a person, place, animal, or higher self that makes you feel safe and loved: **Imagine** and feel this essence. Soften your gaze/or close your eyes and take a few deep breaths as you connect. **Feel** and sense the loving, caring, and safe contact. Allow yourself to **melt** into the most soothing and comforting embrace. Allow yourself to **stay here for a full minute.** Is there a **sensation** or a **message** that comes to you? **Where** do you feel it in your body? *List the words that best describe this experience:*
_____
_____
_____
_____

Identify one thing you are **grateful** for today: Make sure it's different from what you identified yesterday. [Even the smallest things count] Soften your gaze/or close your eyes and take a few deep breaths as you **take a full minute** to **savor** this feeling of gratitude. *Write the details below:*
_____
_____
_____

Identify a current **need**. Go inside and ask yourself "what do I need?" *Write in third person "your name needs":*
_____
_____
_____

Starting My Day _____/_____/_____

Clear out some mental space. *Briefly describe the strongest thought or stressor that is on your mind – Label the emotion.*

_____

_____

_____

Body Location: _____ Body Sensation: _____

RVRR Part 1: Take a minute to perform part 1 of the RVRR technique. Now, set a plan for when, where and how you will release your vault later today. *Write your plan below:*

_____

_____

_____

Picture just one aspect of your ultimate dream life: Do not plan or strategize about how it's going to happen. **Just picture the final result**. Soften your gaze/or close your eyes and take a few deep breaths as you imagine and connect this part of your ultimate dream life. **Take a full minute** to **enjoy** this experience. How does this part of your ultimate dream life look and feel? *Write the words "What if...?" and then describe this specific aspect of your ultimate dream life.*

_____

_____

_____

_____

_____

Look deep into yourself: See and feel who you are at your core - your values, essence, innate abilities, and your heart. What images and qualities represent the real you? **Affirm** your unique personality. *List the words that best describe you:*

_____

_____

_____

_____

@QuantumMindframe

Ending My Day _____/_____/_____

List two things that went your way today. [Even the smallest things are good to notice]

1._____

2._____

RVRR Part 2: Did you release your vault? How did it go? *Write about it here:*

_____
_____

Visualize a person, place, animal, or higher self that makes you feel safe and loved: **Imagine** and feel this essence. Soften your gaze/or close your eyes and take a few deep breaths as you connect. **Feel** and sense the loving, caring, and safe contact. Allow yourself to **melt** into the most soothing and comforting embrace. Allow yourself to **stay here for a full minute**. Is there a **sensation** or a **message** that comes to you? **Where** do you feel it in your body? *List the words that best describe this experience:*

_____
_____
_____

Identify one thing you are **grateful** for today: Make sure it's different from what you identified yesterday. [Even the smallest things count] Soften your gaze/or close your eyes and take a few deep breaths as you **take a full minute** to **savor** this feeling of gratitude. *Write the details below:*

_____
_____
_____

Identify a current **need**. Go inside and ask yourself "what do I need?" *Write in third person "your name needs":*

_____
_____
_____

Starting My Day _____/_____/_____

Clear out some mental space. *Briefly describe the strongest thought or stressor that is on your mind – Label the emotion.*

_____

_____

_____

Body Location: _____ Body Sensation: _____

RVRR Part 1: Take a minute to perform part 1 of the RVRR technique. Now, set a plan for when, where and how you will release your vault later today. *Write your plan below:*

_____

_____

_____

Picture just one aspect of your ultimate dream life: Do not plan or strategize about how it's going to happen. **Just picture the final result**. Soften your gaze/or close your eyes and take a few deep breaths as you imagine and connect this part of your ultimate dream life. **Take a full minute** to **enjoy** this experience. How does this part of your ultimate dream life look and feel? *Write the words "What if…?" and then describe this specific aspect of your ultimate dream life.*

_____

_____

_____

_____

_____

Look deep into yourself: See and feel who you are at your core - your values, essence, innate abilities, and your heart. What images and qualities represent the real you? **Affirm** your unique personality. *List the words that best describe you:*

_____

_____

_____

_____

Ending My Day _____/_____/_____

List two things that went your way today. [Even the smallest things are good to notice]

1._____

2._____

RVRR Part 2: Did you release your vault? How did it go? *Write about it here:*
_____
_____

Visualize a person, place, animal, or higher self that makes you feel safe and loved: **Imagine** and feel this essence. Soften your gaze/or close your eyes and take a few deep breaths as you connect. **Feel** and sense the loving, caring, and safe contact. Allow yourself to **melt** into the most soothing and comforting embrace. Allow yourself to **stay here for a full minute.** Is there a **sensation** or a **message** that comes to you? **Where** do you feel it in your body? *List the words that best describe this experience:*
_____
_____
_____

Identify one thing you are **grateful** for today: Make sure it's different from what you identified yesterday. [Even the smallest things count] Soften your gaze/or close your eyes and take a few deep breaths as you **take a full minute** to **savor** this feeling of gratitude. *Write the details below:*
_____
_____
_____

Identify a current **need**. Go inside and ask yourself "what do I need?" *Write in third person "your name needs":*
_____
_____

Starting My Day _____/_____/_____

Clear out some mental space. *Briefly describe the strongest thought or stressor that is on your mind – Label the emotion.*

_____

_____

_____

Body Location: _____ Body Sensation: _____

RVRR Part 1: Take a minute to perform part 1 of the RVRR technique. Now, set a plan for when, where and how you will release your vault later today. *Write your plan below:*

_____

_____

_____

Picture just one aspect of your ultimate dream life: Do not plan or strategize about how it's going to happen. **Just picture the final result**. Soften your gaze/or close your eyes and take a few deep breaths as you imagine and connect this part of your ultimate dream life. **Take a full minute** to **enjoy** this experience. How does this part of your ultimate dream life look and feel? *Write the words "What if…?" and then describe this specific aspect of your ultimate dream life.*

_____

_____

_____

_____

_____

Look deep into yourself: See and feel who you are at your core - your values, essence, innate abilities, and your heart. What images and qualities represent the real you? **Affirm** your unique personality. *List the words that best describe you:*

_____

_____

_____

_____

Ending My Day _____/_____/_____

List two things that went your way today. [Even the smallest things are good to notice]

1._____

2._____

RVRR Part 2: Did you release your vault? How did it go? *Write about it here:*
_____
_____
_____

Visualize a person, place, animal, or higher self that makes you feel safe and loved: **Imagine** and feel this essence. Soften your gaze/or close your eyes and take a few deep breaths as you connect. **Feel** and sense the loving, caring, and safe contact. Allow yourself to **melt** into the most soothing and comforting embrace. Allow yourself to **stay here for a full minute**. Is there a **sensation** or a **message** that comes to you? **Where** do you feel it in your body? *List the words that best describe this experience:*
_____
_____
_____
_____

Identify one thing you are **grateful** for today: Make sure it's different from what you identified yesterday. [Even the smallest things count] Soften your gaze/or close your eyes and take a few deep breaths as you **take a full minute** to **savor** this feeling of gratitude. *Write the details below:*
_____
_____
_____

Identify a current **need**. Go inside and ask yourself "what do I need?" *Write in third person "your name needs":*
_____
_____
_____

Starting My Day _____/_____/_____

Clear out some mental space. *Briefly describe the strongest thought or stressor that is on your mind – Label the emotion.*

_____

_____

_____

Body Location: _____ Body Sensation: _____

RVRR Part 1: Take a minute to perform part 1 of the RVRR technique. Now, set a plan for when, where and how you will release your vault later today. *Write your plan below:*

_____

_____

_____

Picture just one aspect of your ultimate dream life: Do not plan or strategize about how it's going to happen. **Just picture the final result**. Soften your gaze/or close your eyes and take a few deep breaths as you imagine and connect this part of your ultimate dream life. **Take a full minute** to **enjoy** this experience. How does this part of your ultimate dream life look and feel? *Write the words "What if…?" and then describe this specific aspect of your ultimate dream life.*

_____

_____

_____

_____

_____

Look deep into yourself: See and feel who you are at your core - your values, essence, innate abilities, and your heart. What images and qualities represent the real you? **Affirm** your unique personality. *List the words that best describe you:*

_____

_____

_____

_____

Ending My Day _____ / _____ / _____

List two things that went your way today. [Even the smallest things are good to notice]

1._____

2._____

RVRR Part 2: Did you release your vault? How did it go? *Write about it here:*
_____
_____
_____

Visualize a person, place, animal, or higher self that makes you feel safe and loved: **Imagine** and feel this essence. Soften your gaze/or close your eyes and take a few deep breaths as you connect. **Feel** and sense the loving, caring, and safe contact. Allow yourself to **melt** into the most soothing and comforting embrace. Allow yourself to **stay here for a full minute.** Is there a **sensation** or a **message** that comes to you? **Where** do you feel it in your body? *List the words that best describe this experience:*
_____
_____
_____
_____

Identify one thing you are **grateful** for today: Make sure it's different from what you identified yesterday. [Even the smallest things count] Soften your gaze/or close your eyes and take a few deep breaths as you **take a full minute** to **savor** this feeling of gratitude. *Write the details below:*
_____
_____
_____

Identify a current **need**. Go inside and ask yourself "what do I need?" *Write in third person "your name needs":*
_____
_____
_____

Starting My Day _____/_____/_____

Clear out some mental space. *Briefly describe the strongest thought or stressor that is on your mind – Label the emotion.*

_____

_____

_____

Body Location: _____ Body Sensation: _____

RVRR Part 1: Take a minute to perform part 1 of the RVRR technique. Now, set a plan for when, where and how you will release your vault later today. *Write your plan below:*

_____

_____

_____

Picture just one aspect of your ultimate dream life: Do not plan or strategize about how it's going to happen. **Just picture the final result**. Soften your gaze/or close your eyes and take a few deep breaths as you imagine and connect this part of your ultimate dream life. **Take a full minute** to **enjoy** this experience. How does this part of your ultimate dream life look and feel? *Write the words "What if…?" and then describe this specific aspect of your ultimate dream life.*

_____

_____

_____

_____

_____

Look deep into yourself: See and feel who you are at your core - your values, essence, innate abilities, and your heart. What images and qualities represent the real you? **Affirm** your unique personality. *List the words that best describe you:*

_____

_____

_____

_____

Ending My Day _____/_____/_____

List two things that went your way today. [Even the smallest things are good to notice]

1._____

2._____

RVRR Part 2: Did you release your vault? How did it go? *Write about it here:*

_____

_____

_____

Visualize a person, place, animal, or higher self that makes you feel safe and loved: **Imagine** and feel this essence. Soften your gaze/or close your eyes and take a few deep breaths as you connect. **Feel** and sense the loving, caring, and safe contact. Allow yourself to **melt** into the most soothing and comforting embrace. Allow yourself to **stay here for a full minute**. Is there a **sensation** or a **message** that comes to you? **Where** do you feel it in your body? *List the words that best describe this experience:*

_____

_____

_____

_____

Identify one thing you are **grateful** for today: Make sure it's different from what you identified yesterday. [Even the smallest things count] Soften your gaze/or close your eyes and take a few deep breaths as you **take a full minute** to **savor** this feeling of gratitude. *Write the details below:*

_____

_____

_____

Identify a current **need**. Go inside and ask yourself "what do I need?" *Write in third person "your name needs":*

_____

_____

_____

Starting My Day _____ / _____ / _____

Clear out some mental space. *Briefly describe the strongest thought or stressor that is on your mind – Label the emotion.*

_____

_____

_____

Body Location: _____ Body Sensation: _____

RVRR Part 1: Take a minute to perform part 1 of the RVRR technique. Now, set a plan for when, where and how you will release your vault later today. *Write your plan below:*

_____

_____

_____

Picture just one aspect of your ultimate dream life: Do not plan or strategize about how it's going to happen. **Just picture the final result.** Soften your gaze/or close your eyes and take a few deep breaths as you imagine and connect this part of your ultimate dream life. **Take a full minute** to **enjoy** this experience. How does this part of your ultimate dream life look and feel? *Write the words "What if...?" and then describe this specific aspect of your ultimate dream life.*

_____

_____

_____

_____

_____

Look deep into yourself: See and feel who you are at your core - your values, essence, innate abilities, and your heart. What images and qualities represent the real you? **Affirm** your unique personality. *List the words that best describe you:*

_____

_____

_____

_____

Ending My Day _____/_____/_____

List two things that went your way today. [Even the smallest things are good to notice]

1._____

2._____

RVRR Part 2: Did you release your vault? How did it go? *Write about it here:*

_____

_____

_____

Visualize a person, place, animal, or higher self that makes you feel safe and loved: **Imagine** and feel this essence. Soften your gaze/or close your eyes and take a few deep breaths as you connect. **Feel** and sense the loving, caring, and safe contact. Allow yourself to **melt** into the most soothing and comforting embrace. Allow yourself to **stay here for a full minute**. Is there a **sensation** or a **message** that comes to you? **Where** do you feel it in your body? *List the words that best describe this experience:*

_____

_____

_____

_____

Identify one thing you are **grateful** for today: Make sure it's different from what you identified yesterday. [Even the smallest things count] Soften your gaze/or close your eyes and take a few deep breaths as you **take a full minute** to **savor** this feeling of gratitude. *Write the details below:*

_____

_____

_____

Identify a current **need**. Go inside and ask yourself "what do I need?" *Write in third person "your name needs":*

_____

_____

_____

Starting My Day _____/_____/_____

Clear out some mental space. *Briefly describe the strongest thought or stressor that is on your mind – Label the emotion.*

_____

Body Location: _____ Body Sensation: _____

RVRR Part 1: Take a minute to perform part 1 of the RVRR technique. Now, set a plan for when, where and how you will release your vault later today. *Write your plan below:*

_____

Picture just one aspect of your ultimate dream life: Do not plan or strategize about how it's going to happen. **Just picture the final result**. Soften your gaze/or close your eyes and take a few deep breaths as you imagine and connect this part of your ultimate dream life. **Take a full minute** to **enjoy** this experience. How does this part of your ultimate dream life look and feel? *Write the words "What if…?" and then describe this specific aspect of your ultimate dream life.*

_____

Look deep into yourself: See and feel who you are at your core - your values, essence, innate abilities, and your heart. What images and qualities represent the real you? **Affirm** your unique personality. *List the words that best describe you:*

_____

Ending My Day _____/_____/_____

List two things that went your way today. [Even the smallest things are good to notice]

1._____

2._____

RVRR Part 2: Did you release your vault? How did it go? *Write about it here:*
_____
_____

Visualize a person, place, animal, or higher self that makes you feel safe and loved: **Imagine** and feel this essence. Soften your gaze/or close your eyes and take a few deep breaths as you connect. **Feel** and sense the loving, caring, and safe contact. Allow yourself to **melt** into the most soothing and comforting embrace. Allow yourself to **stay here for a full minute**. Is there a **sensation** or a **message** that comes to you? **Where** do you feel it in your body? *List the words that best describe this experience:*
_____
_____
_____

Identify one thing you are **grateful** for today: Make sure it's different from what you identified yesterday. [Even the smallest things count] Soften your gaze/or close your eyes and take a few deep breaths as you **take a full minute** to **savor** this feeling of gratitude. *Write the details below:*
_____
_____

Identify a current **need**. Go inside and ask yourself "what do I need?" *Write in third person "your name needs":*
_____
_____

Starting My Day _____/_____/_____

Clear out some mental space. *Briefly describe the strongest thought or stressor that is on your mind – Label the emotion.*

_____

_____

_____

Body Location: _____ Body Sensation: _____

RVRR Part 1: Take a minute to perform part 1 of the RVRR technique. Now, set a plan for when, where and how you will release your vault later today. *Write your plan below:*

_____

_____

_____

Picture just one aspect of your ultimate dream life: Do not plan or strategize about how it's going to happen. **Just picture the final result**. Soften your gaze/or close your eyes and take a few deep breaths as you imagine and connect this part of your ultimate dream life. **Take a full minute** to **enjoy** this experience. How does this part of your ultimate dream life look and feel? *Write the words "What if…?" and then describe this specific aspect of your ultimate dream life.*

_____

_____

_____

_____

_____

Look deep into yourself: See and feel who you are at your core - your values, essence, innate abilities, and your heart. What images and qualities represent the real you? **Affirm** your unique personality. *List the words that best describe you:*

_____

_____

_____

_____

@QuantumMindframe

Ending My Day _____/_____/_____

List two things that went your way today. [Even the smallest things are good to notice]

1._____

2._____

RVRR Part 2: Did you release your vault? How did it go? *Write about it here:*
_____
_____

Visualize a person, place, animal, or higher self that makes you feel safe and loved: **Imagine** and feel this essence. Soften your gaze/or close your eyes and take a few deep breaths as you connect. **Feel** and sense the loving, caring, and safe contact. Allow yourself to **melt** into the most soothing and comforting embrace. Allow yourself to **stay here for a full minute.** Is there a **sensation** or a **message** that comes to you? **Where** do you feel it in your body? *List the words that best describe this experience:*
_____
_____
_____

Identify one thing you are **grateful** for today: Make sure it's different from what you identified yesterday. [Even the smallest things count] Soften your gaze/or close your eyes and take a few deep breaths as you **take a full minute** to **savor** this feeling of gratitude. *Write the details below:*
_____
_____

Identify a current **need**. Go inside and ask yourself "what do I need?" *Write in third person "your name needs":*
_____
_____

Starting My Day _____/_____/_____

Clear out some mental space. *Briefly describe the strongest thought or stressor that is on your mind – Label the emotion.*

_____

_____

_____

Body Location: _____ Body Sensation: _____

RVRR Part 1: Take a minute to perform part 1 of the RVRR technique. Now, set a plan for when, where and how you will release your vault later today. *Write your plan below:*

_____

_____

_____

Picture just one aspect of your ultimate dream life: Do not plan or strategize about how it's going to happen. **Just picture the final result.** Soften your gaze/or close your eyes and take a few deep breaths as you imagine and connect this part of your ultimate dream life. **Take a full minute** to **enjoy** this experience. How does this part of your ultimate dream life look and feel? *Write the words "What if…?" and then describe this specific aspect of your ultimate dream life.*

_____

_____

_____

_____

_____

Look deep into yourself: See and feel who you are at your core - your values, essence, innate abilities, and your heart. What images and qualities represent the real you? **Affirm** your unique personality. *List the words that best describe you:*

_____

_____

_____

_____

Ending My Day _____/_____/_____

List two things that went your way today. [Even the smallest things are good to notice]

1._____

2._____

RVRR Part 2: Did you release your vault? How did it go? *Write about it here:*

_____

_____

Visualize a person, place, animal, or higher self that makes you feel safe and loved: **Imagine** and feel this essence. Soften your gaze/or close your eyes and take a few deep breaths as you connect. **Feel** and sense the loving, caring, and safe contact. Allow yourself to **melt** into the most soothing and comforting embrace. Allow yourself to **stay here for a full minute**. Is there a **sensation** or a **message** that comes to you? **Where** do you feel it in your body? *List the words that best describe this experience:*

_____

_____

_____

Identify one thing you are **grateful** for today: Make sure it's different from what you identified yesterday. [Even the smallest things count] Soften your gaze/or close your eyes and take a few deep breaths as you **take a full minute** to **savor** this feeling of gratitude. *Write the details below:*

_____

_____

Identify a current **need**. Go inside and ask yourself "what do I need?" *Write in third person "your name needs":*

_____

_____

Starting My Day _____/_____/_____

Clear out some mental space. *Briefly describe the strongest thought or stressor that is on your mind – Label the emotion.*

_____

_____

Body Location: _____ Body Sensation: _____

RVRR Part 1: Take a minute to perform part 1 of the RVRR technique. Now, set a plan for when, where and how you will release your vault later today. *Write your plan below:*

_____

_____

_____

Picture just one aspect of your ultimate dream life: Do not plan or strategize about how it's going to happen. **Just picture the final result**. Soften your gaze/or close your eyes and take a few deep breaths as you imagine and connect this part of your ultimate dream life. **Take a full minute** to **enjoy** this experience. How does this part of your ultimate dream life look and feel? *Write the words "What if...?" and then describe this specific aspect of your ultimate dream life.*

_____

_____

_____

_____

_____

Look deep into yourself: See and feel who you are at your core - your values, essence, innate abilities, and your heart. What images and qualities represent the real you? **Affirm** your unique personality. *List the words that best describe you:*

_____

_____

_____

_____

Ending My Day _____/_____/_____

List two things that went your way today. [Even the smallest things are good to notice]

1._____

2._____

RVRR Part 2: Did you release your vault? How did it go? *Write about it here:*
_____
_____
_____

Visualize a person, place, animal, or higher self that makes you feel safe and loved: **Imagine** and feel this essence. Soften your gaze/or close your eyes and take a few deep breaths as you connect. **Feel** and sense the loving, caring, and safe contact. Allow yourself to **melt** into the most soothing and comforting embrace. Allow yourself to **stay here for a full minute**. Is there a **sensation** or a **message** that comes to you? **Where** do you feel it in your body? *List the words that best describe this experience:*
_____
_____
_____

Identify one thing you are **grateful** for today: Make sure it's different from what you identified yesterday. [Even the smallest things count] Soften your gaze/or close your eyes and take a few deep breaths as you **take a full minute** to **savor** this feeling of gratitude. *Write the details below:*
_____
_____
_____

Identify a current **need**. Go inside and ask yourself "what do I need?" *Write in third person "your name needs":*
_____
_____
_____

Starting My Day _____/_____/_____

Clear out some mental space. *Briefly describe the strongest thought or stressor that is on your mind – Label the emotion.*

_____
_____
_____

Body Location: _____ Body Sensation: _____

RVRR Part 1: Take a minute to perform part 1 of the RVRR technique. Now, set a plan for when, where and how you will release your vault later today. *Write your plan below:*

_____
_____
_____

Picture just one aspect of your ultimate dream life: Do not plan or strategize about how it's going to happen. **Just picture the final result.** Soften your gaze/or close your eyes and take a few deep breaths as you imagine and connect this part of your ultimate dream life. **Take a full minute** to **enjoy** this experience. How does this part of your ultimate dream life look and feel? *Write the words "What if...?" and then describe this specific aspect of your ultimate dream life.*

_____
_____
_____
_____
_____

Look deep into yourself: See and feel who you are at your core - your values, essence, innate abilities, and your heart. What images and qualities represent the real you? **Affirm** your unique personality. *List the words that best describe you:*

_____
_____
_____
_____

Ending My Day _____/_____/_____

List two things that went your way today. [Even the smallest things are good to notice]

1._____

2._____

RVRR Part 2: Did you release your vault? How did it go? *Write about it here:*
_____
_____
_____

Visualize a person, place, animal, or higher self that makes you feel safe and loved: **Imagine** and feel this essence. Soften your gaze/or close your eyes and take a few deep breaths as you connect. **Feel** and sense the loving, caring, and safe contact. Allow yourself to **melt** into the most soothing and comforting embrace. Allow yourself to **stay here for a full minute**. Is there a **sensation** or a **message** that comes to you? **Where** do you feel it in your body? *List the words that best describe this experience:*
_____
_____
_____

Identify one thing you are **grateful** for today: Make sure it's different from what you identified yesterday. [Even the smallest things count] Soften your gaze/or close your eyes and take a few deep breaths as you **take a full minute** to **savor** this feeling of gratitude. *Write the details below:*
_____
_____
_____

Identify a current **need**. Go inside and ask yourself "what do I need?" *Write in third person "your name needs":*
_____
_____
_____

Starting My Day _____/_____/_____

Clear out some mental space. *Briefly describe the strongest thought or stressor that is on your mind – Label the emotion.*

_____

_____

_____

Body Location: _____ Body Sensation: _____

RVRR Part 1: Take a minute to perform part 1 of the RVRR technique. Now, set a plan for when, where and how you will release your vault later today. *Write your plan below:*

_____

_____

_____

Picture just one aspect of your ultimate dream life: Do not plan or strategize about how it's going to happen. **Just picture the final result.** Soften your gaze/or close your eyes and take a few deep breaths as you imagine and connect this part of your ultimate dream life. **Take a full minute** to **enjoy** this experience. How does this part of your ultimate dream life look and feel? *Write the words "What if...?" and then describe this specific aspect of your ultimate dream life.*

_____

_____

_____

_____

_____

Look deep into yourself: See and feel who you are at your core - your values, essence, innate abilities, and your heart. What images and qualities represent the real you? **Affirm** your unique personality. *List the words that best describe you:*

_____

_____

_____

_____

Ending My Day _____/_____/_____

List two things that went your way today. [Even the smallest things are good to notice]

1._____

2._____

RVRR Part 2: Did you release your vault? How did it go? *Write about it here:*

_____

_____

Visualize a person, place, animal, or higher self that makes you feel safe and loved: **Imagine** and feel this essence. Soften your gaze/or close your eyes and take a few deep breaths as you connect. **Feel** and sense the loving, caring, and safe contact. Allow yourself to **melt** into the most soothing and comforting embrace. Allow yourself to **stay here for a full minute**. Is there a **sensation** or a **message** that comes to you? **Where** do you feel it in your body? *List the words that best describe this experience:*

_____

_____

_____

Identify one thing you are **grateful** for today: Make sure it's different from what you identified yesterday. [Even the smallest things count] Soften your gaze/or close your eyes and take a few deep breaths as you **take a full minute** to **savor** this feeling of gratitude. *Write the details below:*

_____

_____

_____

Identify a current **need**. Go inside and ask yourself "what do I need?" *Write in third person "your name needs":*

_____

_____

_____

Starting My Day _____/_____/_____

Clear out some mental space. *Briefly describe the strongest thought or stressor that is on your mind – Label the emotion.*

_____

_____

_____

Body Location: _____ Body Sensation: _____

RVRR Part 1: Take a minute to perform part 1 of the RVRR technique. Now, set a plan for when, where and how you will release your vault later today. *Write your plan below:*

_____

_____

_____

Picture just one aspect of your ultimate dream life: Do not plan or strategize about how it's going to happen. **Just picture the final result.** Soften your gaze/or close your eyes and take a few deep breaths as you imagine and connect this part of your ultimate dream life. **Take a full minute** to **enjoy** this experience. How does this part of your ultimate dream life look and feel? *Write the words "What if...?" and then describe this specific aspect of your ultimate dream life.*

_____

_____

_____

_____

_____

Look deep into yourself: See and feel who you are at your core - your values, essence, innate abilities, and your heart. What images and qualities represent the real you? **Affirm** your unique personality. *List the words that best describe you:*

_____

_____

_____

_____

_____

@QuantumMindframe

Ending My Day _____/_____/_____

List two things that went your way today. [Even the smallest things are good to notice]

1._____

2._____

RVRR Part 2: Did you release your vault? How did it go? *Write about it here:*

_____

_____

_____

Visualize a person, place, animal, or higher self that makes you feel safe and loved: **Imagine** and feel this essence. Soften your gaze/or close your eyes and take a few deep breaths as you connect. **Feel** and sense the loving, caring, and safe contact. Allow yourself to **melt** into the most soothing and comforting embrace. Allow yourself to **stay here for a full minute**. Is there a **sensation** or a **message** that comes to you? **Where** do you feel it in your body? *List the words that best describe this experience:*

_____

_____

_____

Identify one thing you are **grateful** for today: Make sure it's different from what you identified yesterday. [Even the smallest things count] Soften your gaze/or close your eyes and take a few deep breaths as you **take a full minute** to **savor** this feeling of gratitude. *Write the details below:*

_____

_____

_____

Identify a current **need**. Go inside and ask yourself "what do I need?" *Write in third person "your name needs":*

_____

_____

_____

Starting My Day _____/_____/_____

Clear out some mental space. *Briefly describe the strongest thought or stressor that is on your mind – Label the emotion.*

_____

_____

_____

Body Location: _____ Body Sensation: _____

RVRR Part 1: Take a minute to perform part 1 of the RVRR technique. Now, set a plan for when, where and how you will release your vault later today. *Write your plan below:*

_____

_____

_____

Picture just one aspect of your ultimate dream life: Do not plan or strategize about how it's going to happen. **Just picture the final result**. Soften your gaze/or close your eyes and take a few deep breaths as you imagine and connect this part of your ultimate dream life. **Take a full minute** to **enjoy** this experience. How does this part of your ultimate dream life look and feel? *Write the words "What if...?" and then describe this specific aspect of your ultimate dream life.*

_____

_____

_____

_____

_____

Look deep into yourself: See and feel who you are at your core - your values, essence, innate abilities, and your heart. What images and qualities represent the real you? **Affirm** your unique personality. *List the words that best describe you:*

_____

_____

_____

_____

Ending My Day _____/_____/_____

List two things that went your way today. [Even the smallest things are good to notice]

1._____

2._____

RVRR Part 2: Did you release your vault? How did it go? *Write about it here:*
_____
_____
_____

Visualize a person, place, animal, or higher self that makes you feel safe and loved: **Imagine** and feel this essence. Soften your gaze/or close your eyes and take a few deep breaths as you connect. **Feel** and sense the loving, caring, and safe contact. Allow yourself to **melt** into the most soothing and comforting embrace. Allow yourself to **stay here for a full minute**. Is there a **sensation** or a **message** that comes to you? **Where** do you feel it in your body? *List the words that best describe this experience:*
_____
_____
_____

Identify one thing you are **grateful** for today: Make sure it's different from what you identified yesterday. [Even the smallest things count] Soften your gaze/or close your eyes and take a few deep breaths as you **take a full minute** to **savor** this feeling of gratitude. *Write the details below:*
_____
_____
_____

Identify a current **need**. Go inside and ask yourself "what do I need?" *Write in third person "your name needs":*
_____
_____
_____

Starting My Day _____/_____/_____

Clear out some mental space. *Briefly describe the strongest thought or stressor that is on your mind – Label the emotion.*

_____
_____
_____

Body Location: _____ Body Sensation: _____

RVRR Part 1: Take a minute to perform part 1 of the RVRR technique. Now, set a plan for when, where and how you will release your vault later today. *Write your plan below:*

_____
_____
_____

Picture just one aspect of your ultimate dream life: Do not plan or strategize about how it's going to happen. **Just picture the final result.** Soften your gaze/or close your eyes and take a few deep breaths as you imagine and connect this part of your ultimate dream life. **Take a full minute** to **enjoy** this experience. How does this part of your ultimate dream life look and feel? *Write the words "What if...?" and then describe this specific aspect of your ultimate dream life.*

_____
_____
_____
_____
_____

Look deep into yourself: See and feel who you are at your core – your values, essence, innate abilities, and your heart. What images and qualities represent the real you? **Affirm** your unique personality. *List the words that best describe you:*

_____
_____
_____
_____

Ending My Day _____/_____/_____

List two things that went your way today. [Even the smallest things are good to notice]

1._____
2._____

RVRR Part 2: Did you release your vault? How did it go? *Write about it here:*
_____
_____
_____

Visualize a person, place, animal, or higher self that makes you feel safe and loved: **Imagine** and feel this essence. Soften your gaze/or close your eyes and take a few deep breaths as you connect. **Feel** and sense the loving, caring, and safe contact. Allow yourself to **melt** into the most soothing and comforting embrace. Allow yourself to **stay here for a full minute.** Is there a **sensation** or a **message** that comes to you? **Where** do you feel it in your body? *List the words that best describe this experience:*
_____
_____
_____
_____

Identify one thing you are **grateful** for today: Make sure it's different from what you identified yesterday. [Even the smallest things count] Soften your gaze/or close your eyes and take a few deep breaths as you **take a full minute** to **savor** this feeling of gratitude. *Write the details below:*
_____
_____
_____

Identify a current **need**. Go inside and ask yourself "what do I need?" *Write in third person "your name needs":*
_____
_____
_____

Starting My Day _____/_____/_____

Clear out some mental space. *Briefly describe the strongest thought or stressor that is on your mind – Label the emotion.*

_____

_____

_____

Body Location: _____ Body Sensation: _____

RVRR Part 1: Take a minute to perform part 1 of the RVRR technique. Now, set a plan for when, where and how you will release your vault later today. *Write your plan below:*

_____

_____

_____

Picture just one aspect of your ultimate dream life: Do not plan or strategize about how it's going to happen. **Just picture the final result.** Soften your gaze/or close your eyes and take a few deep breaths as you imagine and connect this part of your ultimate dream life. **Take a full minute** to **enjoy** this experience. How does this part of your ultimate dream life look and feel? *Write the words "What if…?" and then describe this specific aspect of your ultimate dream life.*

_____

_____

_____

_____

_____

Look deep into yourself: See and feel who you are at your core - your values, essence, innate abilities, and your heart. What images and qualities represent the real you? **Affirm** your unique personality. *List the words that best describe you:*

_____

_____

_____

_____

Ending My Day _____/_____/_____

List two things that went your way today. [Even the smallest things are good to notice]

1._____

2._____

RVRR Part 2: Did you release your vault? How did it go? *Write about it here:*
_____
_____
_____

Visualize a person, place, animal, or higher self that makes you feel safe and loved: **Imagine** and feel this essence. Soften your gaze/or close your eyes and take a few deep breaths as you connect. **Feel** and sense the loving, caring, and safe contact. Allow yourself to **melt** into the most soothing and comforting embrace. Allow yourself to **stay here for a full minute.** Is there a **sensation** or a **message** that comes to you? **Where** do you feel it in your body? *List the words that best describe this experience:*
_____
_____
_____

Identify one thing you are **grateful** for today: Make sure it's different from what you identified yesterday. [Even the smallest things count] Soften your gaze/or close your eyes and take a few deep breaths as you **take a full minute** to **savor** this feeling of gratitude. *Write the details below:*
_____
_____
_____

Identify a current **need**. Go inside and ask yourself "what do I need?" *Write in third person "your name needs":*
_____
_____
_____

Starting My Day _____/_____/_____

Clear out some mental space. *Briefly describe the strongest thought or stressor that is on your mind – Label the emotion.*

_____
_____
_____

Body Location: _____ Body Sensation: _____

RVRR Part 1: Take a minute to perform part 1 of the RVRR technique. Now, set a plan for when, where and how you will release your vault later today. *Write your plan below:*

_____
_____
_____

Picture just one aspect of your ultimate dream life: Do not plan or strategize about how it's going to happen. **Just picture the final result.** Soften your gaze/or close your eyes and take a few deep breaths as you imagine and connect this part of your ultimate dream life. **Take a full minute** to **enjoy** this experience. How does this part of your ultimate dream life look and feel? *Write the words "What if…?" and then describe this specific aspect of your ultimate dream life.*

_____
_____
_____
_____
_____

Look deep into yourself: See and feel who you are at your core - your values, essence, innate abilities, and your heart. What images and qualities represent the real you? **Affirm** your unique personality. *List the words that best describe you:*

_____
_____
_____
_____

Ending My Day _____/_____/_____

List two things that went your way today. [Even the smallest things are good to notice]

1._____

2._____

RVRR Part 2: Did you release your vault? How did it go? *Write about it here:*

_____

_____

_____

Visualize a person, place, animal, or higher self that makes you feel safe and loved: **Imagine** and feel this essence. Soften your gaze/or close your eyes and take a few deep breaths as you connect. **Feel** and sense the loving, caring, and safe contact. Allow yourself to **melt** into the most soothing and comforting embrace. Allow yourself to **stay here for a full minute**. Is there a **sensation** or a **message** that comes to you? **Where** do you feel it in your body? *List the words that best describe this experience:*

_____

_____

_____

Identify one thing you are **grateful** for today: Make sure it's different from what you identified yesterday. [Even the smallest things count] Soften your gaze/or close your eyes and take a few deep breaths as you **take a full minute** to **savor** this feeling of gratitude. *Write the details below:*

_____

_____

_____

Identify a current **need**. Go inside and ask yourself "what do I need?" *Write in third person "your name needs":*

_____

_____

_____

Starting My Day _____/_____/_____

Clear out some mental space. *Briefly describe the strongest thought or stressor that is on your mind – Label the emotion.*

_____

_____

_____

Body Location: _____ Body Sensation: _____

RVRR Part 1: Take a minute to perform part 1 of the RVRR technique. Now, set a plan for when, where and how you will release your vault later today. *Write your plan below:*

_____

_____

_____

Picture just one aspect of your ultimate dream life: Do not plan or strategize about how it's going to happen. **Just picture the final result**. Soften your gaze/or close your eyes and take a few deep breaths as you imagine and connect this part of your ultimate dream life. **Take a full minute** to **enjoy** this experience. How does this part of your ultimate dream life look and feel? *Write the words "What if...?" and then describe this specific aspect of your ultimate dream life.*

_____

_____

_____

_____

_____

Look deep into yourself: See and feel who you are at your core - your values, essence, innate abilities, and your heart. What images and qualities represent the real you? **Affirm** your unique personality. *List the words that best describe you:*

_____

_____

_____

_____

Ending My Day _____/_____/_____

List two things that went your way today. [Even the smallest things are good to notice]

1._____

2._____

RVRR Part 2: Did you release your vault? How did it go? *Write about it here:*

_____

_____

_____

Visualize a person, place, animal, or higher self that makes you feel safe and loved: **Imagine** and feel this essence. Soften your gaze/or close your eyes and take a few deep breaths as you connect. **Feel** and sense the loving, caring, and safe contact. Allow yourself to **melt** into the most soothing and comforting embrace. Allow yourself to **stay here for a full minute.** Is there a **sensation** or a **message** that comes to you? **Where** do you feel it in your body? *List the words that best describe this experience:*

_____

_____

_____

_____

Identify one thing you are **grateful** for today: Make sure it's different from what you identified yesterday. [Even the smallest things count] Soften your gaze/or close your eyes and take a few deep breaths as you **take a full minute** to **savor** this feeling of gratitude. *Write the details below:*

_____

_____

_____

Identify a current **need**. Go inside and ask yourself "what do I need?" *Write in third person "your name needs":*

_____

_____

_____

Starting My Day _____/_____/_____

Clear out some mental space. *Briefly describe the strongest thought or stressor that is on your mind – Label the emotion.*

_____

_____

Body Location: _____ Body Sensation: _____

RVRR Part 1: Take a minute to perform part 1 of the RVRR technique. Now, set a plan for when, where and how you will release your vault later today. *Write your plan below:*

_____

_____

_____

Picture just one aspect of your ultimate dream life: Do not plan or strategize about how it's going to happen. **Just picture the final result**. Soften your gaze/or close your eyes and take a few deep breaths as you imagine and connect this part of your ultimate dream life. **Take a full minute** to **enjoy** this experience. How does this part of your ultimate dream life look and feel? *Write the words "What if…?" and then describe this specific aspect of your ultimate dream life.*

_____

_____

_____

_____

Look deep into yourself: See and feel who you are at your core - your values, essence, innate abilities, and your heart. What images and qualities represent the real you? **Affirm** your unique personality. *List the words that best describe you:*

_____

_____

_____

_____

Ending My Day _____/_____/_____

List two things that went your way today. [Even the smallest things are good to notice]

1._____

2._____

RVRR Part 2: Did you release your vault? How did it go? *Write about it here:*

_____

_____

_____

Visualize a person, place, animal, or higher self that makes you feel safe and loved: **Imagine** and feel this essence. Soften your gaze/or close your eyes and take a few deep breaths as you connect. **Feel** and sense the loving, caring, and safe contact. Allow yourself to **melt** into the most soothing and comforting embrace. Allow yourself to **stay here for a full minute**. Is there a **sensation** or a **message** that comes to you? **Where** do you feel it in your body? *List the words that best describe this experience:*

_____

_____

_____

Identify one thing you are **grateful** for today: Make sure it's different from what you identified yesterday. [Even the smallest things count] Soften your gaze/or close your eyes and take a few deep breaths as you **take a full minute** to **savor** this feeling of gratitude. *Write the details below:*

_____

_____

_____

Identify a current **need**. Go inside and ask yourself "what do I need?" *Write in third person "your name needs":*

_____

_____

_____

Starting My Day _____/_____/_____

Clear out some mental space. *Briefly describe the strongest thought or stressor that is on your mind – Label the emotion.*

_____

_____

_____

Body Location: _____ Body Sensation: _____

RVRR Part 1: Take a minute to perform part 1 of the RVRR technique. Now, set a plan for when, where and how you will release your vault later today. *Write your plan below:*

_____

_____

_____

Picture just one aspect of your ultimate dream life: Do not plan or strategize about how it's going to happen. **Just picture the final result**. Soften your gaze/or close your eyes and take a few deep breaths as you imagine and connect this part of your ultimate dream life. **Take a full minute** to **enjoy** this experience. How does this part of your ultimate dream life look and feel? *Write the words "What if...?" and then describe this specific aspect of your ultimate dream life.*

_____

_____

_____

_____

_____

_____

Look deep into yourself: See and feel who you are at your core - your values, essence, innate abilities, and your heart. What images and qualities represent the real you? **Affirm** your unique personality. *List the words that best describe you:*

_____

_____

_____

_____

Ending My Day _____ / _____ / _____

List two things that went your way today. [Even the smallest things are good to notice]

1. _____
2. _____

RVRR Part 2: Did you release your vault? How did it go? *Write about it here:*
_____
_____
_____

Visualize a person, place, animal, or higher self that makes you feel safe and loved: **Imagine** and feel this essence. Soften your gaze/or close your eyes and take a few deep breaths as you connect. **Feel** and sense the loving, caring, and safe contact. Allow yourself to **melt** into the most soothing and comforting embrace. Allow yourself to **stay here for a full minute**. Is there a **sensation** or a **message** that comes to you? **Where** do you feel it in your body? *List the words that best describe this experience:*
_____
_____
_____
_____

Identify one thing you are **grateful** for today: Make sure it's different from what you identified yesterday. [Even the smallest things count] Soften your gaze/or close your eyes and take a few deep breaths as you **take a full minute** to **savor** this feeling of gratitude. *Write the details below:*
_____
_____
_____

Identify a current **need**. Go inside and ask yourself "what do I need?" *Write in third person "your name needs":*
_____
_____
_____

Starting My Day _____/_____/_____

Clear out some mental space. *Briefly describe the strongest thought or stressor that is on your mind – Label the emotion.*

_____
_____
_____

Body Location: _____ Body Sensation: _____

RVRR Part 1: Take a minute to perform part 1 of the RVRR technique. Now, set a plan for when, where and how you will release your vault later today. *Write your plan below:*

_____
_____
_____

Picture just one aspect of your ultimate dream life: Do not plan or strategize about how it's going to happen. **Just picture the final result**. Soften your gaze/or close your eyes and take a few deep breaths as you imagine and connect this part of your ultimate dream life. **Take a full minute** to **enjoy** this experience. How does this part of your ultimate dream life look and feel? *Write the words "What if...?" and then describe this specific aspect of your ultimate dream life.*

_____
_____
_____
_____
_____

Look deep into yourself: See and feel who you are at your core - your values, essence, innate abilities, and your heart. What images and qualities represent the real you? **Affirm** your unique personality. *List the words that best describe you:*

_____
_____
_____
_____

Ending My Day _____/_____/_____

List two things that went your way today. [Even the smallest things are good to notice]

1._____
2._____

RVRR Part 2: Did you release your vault? How did it go? *Write about it here:*

_____
_____
_____

Visualize a person, place, animal, or higher self that makes you feel safe and loved: **Imagine** and feel this essence. Soften your gaze/or close your eyes and take a few deep breaths as you connect. **Feel** and sense the loving, caring, and safe contact. Allow yourself to **melt** into the most soothing and comforting embrace. Allow yourself to **stay here for a full minute**. Is there a **sensation** or a **message** that comes to you? **Where** do you feel it in your body? *List the words that best describe this experience:*

_____
_____
_____

Identify one thing you are **grateful** for today: Make sure it's different from what you identified yesterday. [Even the smallest things count] Soften your gaze/or close your eyes and take a few deep breaths as you **take a full minute** to **savor** this feeling of gratitude. *Write the details below:*

_____
_____
_____

Identify a current **need**. Go inside and ask yourself "what do I need?" *Write in third person "your name needs":*

_____
_____

Starting My Day _____/_____/_____

Clear out some mental space. *Briefly describe the strongest thought or stressor that is on your mind – Label the emotion.*

_____
_____
_____

Body Location: _____ Body Sensation: _____

RVRR Part 1: Take a minute to perform part 1 of the RVRR technique. Now, set a plan for when, where and how you will release your vault later today. *Write your plan below:*

_____
_____
_____

Picture just one aspect of your ultimate dream life: Do not plan or strategize about how it's going to happen. **Just picture the final result**. Soften your gaze/or close your eyes and take a few deep breaths as you imagine and connect this part of your ultimate dream life. **Take a full minute** to **enjoy** this experience. How does this part of your ultimate dream life look and feel? *Write the words "What if…?" and then describe this specific aspect of your ultimate dream life.*

_____
_____
_____
_____
_____

Look deep into yourself: See and feel who you are at your core - your values, essence, innate abilities, and your heart. What images and qualities represent the real you? **Affirm** your unique personality. *List the words that best describe you:*

_____
_____
_____
_____
_____

Ending My Day _____/_____/_____

List two things that went your way today. [Even the smallest things are good to notice]

1._____

2._____

RVRR Part 2: Did you release your vault? How did it go? *Write about it here:*

_____
_____
_____

Visualize a person, place, animal, or higher self that makes you feel safe and loved: **Imagine** and feel this essence. Soften your gaze/or close your eyes and take a few deep breaths as you connect. **Feel** and sense the loving, caring, and safe contact. Allow yourself to **melt** into the most soothing and comforting embrace. Allow yourself to **stay here for a full minute**. Is there a **sensation** or a **message** that comes to you? **Where** do you feel it in your body? *List the words that best describe this experience:*

_____
_____
_____
_____

Identify one thing you are **grateful** for today: Make sure it's different from what you identified yesterday. [Even the smallest things count] Soften your gaze/or close your eyes and take a few deep breaths as you **take a full minute** to **savor** this feeling of gratitude. *Write the details below:*

_____
_____
_____

Identify a current **need**. Go inside and ask yourself "what do I need?" *Write in third person "your name needs":*

_____
_____
_____

Starting My Day _____/_____/_____

Clear out some mental space. *Briefly describe the strongest thought or stressor that is on your mind – Label the emotion.*

_____

_____

_____

Body Location: _____ Body Sensation: _____

RVRR Part 1: Take a minute to perform part 1 of the RVRR technique. Now, set a plan for when, where and how you will release your vault later today. *Write your plan below:*

_____

_____

_____

Picture just one aspect of your ultimate dream life: Do not plan or strategize about how it's going to happen. **Just picture the final result**. Soften your gaze/or close your eyes and take a few deep breaths as you imagine and connect this part of your ultimate dream life. **Take a full minute** to **enjoy** this experience. How does this part of your ultimate dream life look and feel? *Write the words "What if…?" and then describe this specific aspect of your ultimate dream life.*

_____

_____

_____

_____

_____

Look deep into yourself: See and feel who you are at your core - your values, essence, innate abilities, and your heart. What images and qualities represent the real you? **Affirm** your unique personality. *List the words that best describe you:*

_____

_____

_____

_____

Ending My Day _____/_____/_____

List two things that went your way today. [Even the smallest things are good to notice]

1._____

2._____

RVRR Part 2: Did you release your vault? How did it go? *Write about it here:*

_____

_____

Visualize a person, place, animal, or higher self that makes you feel safe and loved: **Imagine** and feel this essence. Soften your gaze/or close your eyes and take a few deep breaths as you connect. **Feel** and sense the loving, caring, and safe contact. Allow yourself to **melt** into the most soothing and comforting embrace. Allow yourself to **stay here for a full minute.** Is there a **sensation** or a **message** that comes to you? **Where** do you feel it in your body? *List the words that best describe this experience:*

_____

_____

_____

Identify one thing you are **grateful** for today: Make sure it's different from what you identified yesterday. [Even the smallest things count] Soften your gaze/or close your eyes and take a few deep breaths as you **take a full minute** to **savor** this feeling of gratitude. *Write the details below:*

_____

_____

_____

Identify a current **need**. Go inside and ask yourself "what do I need?" *Write in third person "your name needs":*

_____

_____

_____

Starting My Day _____/_____/_____

Clear out some mental space. *Briefly describe the strongest thought or stressor that is on your mind – Label the emotion.*

_____
_____
_____

Body Location: _____ Body Sensation: _____

RVRR Part 1: Take a minute to perform part 1 of the RVRR technique. Now, set a plan for when, where and how you will release your vault later today. *Write your plan below:*

_____
_____
_____

Picture just one aspect of your ultimate dream life: Do not plan or strategize about how it's going to happen. **Just picture the final result.** Soften your gaze/or close your eyes and take a few deep breaths as you imagine and connect this part of your ultimate dream life. **Take a full minute** to **enjoy** this experience. How does this part of your ultimate dream life look and feel? *Write the words "What if...?" and then describe this specific aspect of your ultimate dream life.*

_____
_____
_____
_____
_____

Look deep into yourself: See and feel who you are at your core – your values, essence, innate abilities, and your heart. What images and qualities represent the real you? **Affirm** your unique personality. *List the words that best describe you:*

_____
_____
_____
_____

Ending My Day _____/_____/_____

List two things that went your way today. [Even the smallest things are good to notice]

1._____

2._____

RVRR Part 2: Did you release your vault? How did it go? *Write about it here:*
_____
_____

Visualize a person, place, animal, or higher self that makes you feel safe and loved: **Imagine** and feel this essence. Soften your gaze/or close your eyes and take a few deep breaths as you connect. **Feel** and sense the loving, caring, and safe contact. Allow yourself to **melt** into the most soothing and comforting embrace. Allow yourself to **stay here for a full minute.** Is there a **sensation** or a **message** that comes to you? **Where** do you feel it in your body? *List the words that best describe this experience:*
_____
_____
_____
_____

Identify one thing you are **grateful** for today: Make sure it's different from what you identified yesterday. [Even the smallest things count] Soften your gaze/or close your eyes and take a few deep breaths as you **take a full minute** to **savor** this feeling of gratitude. *Write the details below:*
_____
_____
_____

Identify a current **need**. Go inside and ask yourself "what do I need?" *Write in third person "your name needs":*
_____
_____

Starting My Day _____/_____/_____

Clear out some mental space. *Briefly describe the strongest thought or stressor that is on your mind – Label the emotion.*

_____
_____
_____

Body Location: _____ Body Sensation: _____

RVRR Part 1: Take a minute to perform part 1 of the RVRR technique. Now, set a plan for when, where and how you will release your vault later today. *Write your plan below:*

_____
_____
_____

Picture just one aspect of your ultimate dream life: Do not plan or strategize about how it's going to happen. **Just picture the final result**. Soften your gaze/or close your eyes and take a few deep breaths as you imagine and connect this part of your ultimate dream life. **Take a full minute** to **enjoy** this experience. How does this part of your ultimate dream life look and feel? *Write the words "What if…?" and then describe this specific aspect of your ultimate dream life.*

_____
_____
_____
_____
_____

Look deep into yourself: See and feel who you are at your core - your values, essence, innate abilities, and your heart. What images and qualities represent the real you? **Affirm** your unique personality. *List the words that best describe you:*

_____
_____
_____
_____

@QuantumMindframe

Ending My Day _____/_____/_____

List two things that went your way today. [Even the smallest things are good to notice]

1._____

2._____

RVRR Part 2: Did you release your vault? How did it go? *Write about it here:*
_____
_____
_____

Visualize a person, place, animal, or higher self that makes you feel safe and loved: **Imagine** and feel this essence. Soften your gaze/or close your eyes and take a few deep breaths as you connect. **Feel** and sense the loving, caring, and safe contact. Allow yourself to **melt** into the most soothing and comforting embrace. Allow yourself to **stay here for a full minute.** Is there a **sensation** or a **message** that comes to you? **Where** do you feel it in your body? *List the words that best describe this experience:*
_____
_____
_____
_____

Identify one thing you are **grateful** for today: Make sure it's different from what you identified yesterday. [Even the smallest things count] Soften your gaze/or close your eyes and take a few deep breaths as you **take a full minute** to **savor** this feeling of gratitude. *Write the details below:*
_____
_____
_____

Identify a current **need**. Go inside and ask yourself "what do I need?" *Write in third person "your name needs":*
_____
_____
_____

Starting My Day _____/_____/_____

Clear out some mental space. *Briefly describe the strongest thought or stressor that is on your mind – Label the emotion.*

_____

_____

Body Location: _____ Body Sensation: _____

RVRR Part 1: Take a minute to perform part 1 of the RVRR technique. Now, set a plan for when, where and how you will release your vault later today. *Write your plan below:*

_____

_____

_____

Picture just one aspect of your ultimate dream life: Do not plan or strategize about how it's going to happen. **Just picture the final result**. Soften your gaze/or close your eyes and take a few deep breaths as you imagine and connect this part of your ultimate dream life. **Take a full minute** to **enjoy** this experience. How does this part of your ultimate dream life look and feel? *Write the words "What if…?" and then describe this specific aspect of your ultimate dream life.*

_____

_____

_____

_____

_____

Look deep into yourself: See and feel who you are at your core - your values, essence, innate abilities, and your heart. What images and qualities represent the real you? **Affirm** your unique personality. *List the words that best describe you:*

_____

_____

_____

_____

Ending My Day _____/_____/_____

List two things that went your way today. [Even the smallest things are good to notice]

1._____

2._____

RVRR Part 2: Did you release your vault? How did it go? *Write about it here:*

_____

_____

_____

Visualize a person, place, animal, or higher self that makes you feel safe and loved: **Imagine** and feel this essence. Soften your gaze/or close your eyes and take a few deep breaths as you connect. **Feel** and sense the loving, caring, and safe contact. Allow yourself to **melt** into the most soothing and comforting embrace. Allow yourself to **stay here for a full minute.** Is there a **sensation** or a **message** that comes to you? **Where** do you feel it in your body? *List the words that best describe this experience:*

_____

_____

_____

_____

Identify one thing you are **grateful** for today: Make sure it's different from what you identified yesterday. [Even the smallest things count] Soften your gaze/or close your eyes and take a few deep breaths as you **take a full minute** to **savor** this feeling of gratitude. *Write the details below:*

_____

_____

_____

Identify a current **need**. Go inside and ask yourself "what do I need?" *Write in third person "your name needs":*

_____

_____

_____

Starting My Day _____/_____/_____

Clear out some mental space. *Briefly describe the strongest thought or stressor that is on your mind – Label the emotion.*

_____

_____

_____

Body Location: _____ Body Sensation: _____

RVRR Part 1: Take a minute to perform part 1 of the RVRR technique. Now, set a plan for when, where and how you will release your vault later today. *Write your plan below:*

_____

_____

_____

Picture just one aspect of your ultimate dream life: Do not plan or strategize about how it's going to happen. **Just picture the final result.** Soften your gaze/or close your eyes and take a few deep breaths as you imagine and connect this part of your ultimate dream life. **Take a full minute** to **enjoy** this experience. How does this part of your ultimate dream life look and feel? *Write the words "What if…?" and then describe this specific aspect of your ultimate dream life.*

_____

_____

_____

_____

_____

Look deep into yourself: See and feel who you are at your core - your values, essence, innate abilities, and your heart. What images and qualities represent the real you? **Affirm** your unique personality. *List the words that best describe you:*

_____

_____

_____

_____

Ending My Day _____/_____/_____

List two things that went your way today. [Even the smallest things are good to notice]

1._____

2._____

RVRR Part 2: Did you release your vault? How did it go? *Write about it here:*

_____

_____

Visualize a person, place, animal, or higher self that makes you feel safe and loved: **Imagine** and feel this essence. Soften your gaze/or close your eyes and take a few deep breaths as you connect. **Feel** and sense the loving, caring, and safe contact. Allow yourself to **melt** into the most soothing and comforting embrace. Allow yourself to **stay here for a full minute**. Is there a **sensation** or a **message** that comes to you? **Where** do you feel it in your body? *List the words that best describe this experience:*

_____

_____

_____

Identify one thing you are **grateful** for today: Make sure it's different from what you identified yesterday. [Even the smallest things count] Soften your gaze/or close your eyes and take a few deep breaths as you **take a full minute** to **savor** this feeling of gratitude. *Write the details below:*

_____

_____

Identify a current **need**. Go inside and ask yourself "what do I need?" *Write in third person "your name needs":*

_____

_____

Starting My Day _____/_____/_____

Clear out some mental space. *Briefly describe the strongest thought or stressor that is on your mind – Label the emotion.*

_____

_____

_____

Body Location: _____ Body Sensation: _____

RVRR Part 1: Take a minute to perform part 1 of the RVRR technique. Now, set a plan for when, where and how you will release your vault later today. *Write your plan below:*

_____

_____

_____

Picture just one aspect of your ultimate dream life: Do not plan or strategize about how it's going to happen. **Just picture the final result**. Soften your gaze/or close your eyes and take a few deep breaths as you imagine and connect this part of your ultimate dream life. **Take a full minute** to **enjoy** this experience. How does this part of your ultimate dream life look and feel? *Write the words "What if…?" and then describe this specific aspect of your ultimate dream life.*

_____

_____

_____

_____

_____

Look deep into yourself: See and feel who you are at your core - your values, essence, innate abilities, and your heart. What images and qualities represent the real you? **Affirm** your unique personality. *List the words that best describe you:*

_____

_____

_____

_____

Ending My Day _____/_____/_____

List two things that went your way today. [Even the smallest things are good to notice]

1._____

2._____

RVRR Part 2: Did you release your vault? How did it go? *Write about it here:*

_____

_____

_____

Visualize a person, place, animal, or higher self that makes you feel safe and loved: **Imagine** and feel this essence. Soften your gaze/or close your eyes and take a few deep breaths as you connect. **Feel** and sense the loving, caring, and safe contact. Allow yourself to **melt** into the most soothing and comforting embrace. Allow yourself to **stay here for a full minute.** Is there a **sensation** or a **message** that comes to you? **Where** do you feel it in your body? *List the words that best describe this experience:*

_____

_____

_____

_____

Identify one thing you are **grateful** for today: Make sure it's different from what you identified yesterday. [Even the smallest things count] Soften your gaze/or close your eyes and take a few deep breaths as you **take a full minute** to **savor** this feeling of gratitude. *Write the details below:*

_____

_____

_____

Identify a current **need**. Go inside and ask yourself "what do I need?" *Write in third person "your name needs":*

_____

_____

_____

Starting My Day _____ / _____ / _____

Clear out some mental space. *Briefly describe the strongest thought or stressor that is on your mind – Label the emotion.*

_____
_____
_____

Body Location: _____ Body Sensation: _____

RVRR Part 1: Take a minute to perform part 1 of the RVRR technique. Now, set a plan for when, where and how you will release your vault later today. *Write your plan below:*

_____
_____
_____

Picture just one aspect of your ultimate dream life: Do not plan or strategize about how it's going to happen. **Just picture the final result**. Soften your gaze/or close your eyes and take a few deep breaths as you imagine and connect this part of your ultimate dream life. **Take a full minute** to **enjoy** this experience. How does this part of your ultimate dream life look and feel? *Write the words "What if…?" and then describe this specific aspect of your ultimate dream life.*

_____
_____
_____
_____
_____

Look deep into yourself: See and feel who you are at your core - your values, essence, innate abilities, and your heart. What images and qualities represent the real you? **Affirm** your unique personality. *List the words that best describe you:*

_____
_____
_____
_____

Ending My Day _____/_____/_____

List two things that went your way today. [Even the smallest things are good to notice]

1._____

2._____

RVRR Part 2: Did you release your vault? How did it go? *Write about it here:*

_____

_____

Visualize a person, place, animal, or higher self that makes you feel safe and loved: **Imagine** and feel this essence. Soften your gaze/or close your eyes and take a few deep breaths as you connect. **Feel** and sense the loving, caring, and safe contact. Allow yourself to **melt** into the most soothing and comforting embrace. Allow yourself to **stay here for a full minute**. Is there a **sensation** or a **message** that comes to you? **Where** do you feel it in your body? *List the words that best describe this experience:*

_____

_____

_____

Identify one thing you are **grateful** for today: Make sure it's different from what you identified yesterday. [Even the smallest things count] Soften your gaze/or close your eyes and take a few deep breaths as you **take a full minute** to **savor** this feeling of gratitude. *Write the details below:*

_____

_____

Identify a current **need**. Go inside and ask yourself "what do I need?" *Write in third person "your name needs":*

_____

_____

Starting My Day _____/_____/_____

Clear out some mental space. *Briefly describe the strongest thought or stressor that is on your mind – Label the emotion.*

_____
_____
_____

Body Location: _____ Body Sensation: _____

RVRR Part 1: Take a minute to perform part 1 of the RVRR technique. Now, set a plan for when, where and how you will release your vault later today. *Write your plan below:*

_____
_____
_____

Picture just one aspect of your ultimate dream life: Do not plan or strategize about how it's going to happen. **Just picture the final result.** Soften your gaze/or close your eyes and take a few deep breaths as you imagine and connect this part of your ultimate dream life. **Take a full minute** to **enjoy** this experience. How does this part of your ultimate dream life look and feel? *Write the words "What if...?" and then describe this specific aspect of your ultimate dream life.*

_____
_____
_____
_____
_____

Look deep into yourself: See and feel who you are at your core - your values, essence, innate abilities, and your heart. What images and qualities represent the real you? **Affirm** your unique personality. *List the words that best describe you:*

_____
_____
_____
_____

Ending My Day _____/_____/_____

List two things that went your way today. [Even the smallest things are good to notice]

1._____

2._____

RVRR Part 2: Did you release your vault? How did it go? *Write about it here:*
_____
_____
_____

Visualize a person, place, animal, or higher self that makes you feel safe and loved: **Imagine** and feel this essence. Soften your gaze/or close your eyes and take a few deep breaths as you connect. **Feel** and sense the loving, caring, and safe contact. Allow yourself to **melt** into the most soothing and comforting embrace. Allow yourself to **stay here for a full minute**. Is there a **sensation** or a **message** that comes to you? **Where** do you feel it in your body? *List the words that best describe this experience:*
_____
_____
_____
_____

Identify one thing you are **grateful** for today: Make sure it's different from what you identified yesterday. [Even the smallest things count] Soften your gaze/or close your eyes and take a few deep breaths as you **take a full minute** to **savor** this feeling of gratitude. *Write the details below:*
_____
_____
_____

Identify a current **need**. Go inside and ask yourself "what do I need?" *Write in third person "your name needs":*
_____
_____
_____

Emotions Glossary

Here is a list of emotions and how they are categorized

Primary Emotions

Primary emotions are the first emotions that people experience in response to a stimulus. They are often universal, basic, and closely linked to survival.

Secondary Emotions

Secondary emotions are emotional responses to primary emotions and are often more complex and nuanced than primary emotions. They can be difficult to understand and usually last longer than primary emotions

Anger

Anger is a primary emotion.

Definition of Anger:
Strong feelings of annoyance, displeasure, or hostility.

Secondary Emotions to Anger:
Disgust, contempt, revulsion, envy, jealousy, exasperation, frustration, irritation, aggravation, agitation, annoyance, grouchiness, grumpiness, rage, bitterness, dislike, ferocity, fury, hate, hostility, loathing, outrage, resentment, scorn, spite, vengefulness, wrath, torment

Fear

Fear is a primary emotion.

Definition of Fear:
An unpleasant emotion caused by the belief that someone or something is dangerous, likely to cause pain, or a threat.

Secondary Emotions to Fear:
Horror, alarm, fright, hysteria, mortification, panic, shock, terror, nervousness, anxiety, apprehension, distress, dread, tenseness, uneasiness, worry

Joy

Joy is a primary emotion.

Definition of Joy:
A feeling of great pleasure and happiness.

Secondary Emotions to Joy:
Cheerfulness, amusement, bliss, delight, ecstasy, elation, enjoyment, euphoria, gaiety, gladness, glee, happiness, jolliness, joviality, joy, jubilation, satisfaction, contentment, pleasure, enthrallment, optimism, eagerness, hope, pride, triumph, relief, zest, enthusiasm, excitement, exhilaration, thrill, zeal

Love

Love is a primary emotion.

Definition of Love:
An intense feeling of deep affection.

Secondary Emotions to Love:
Affection, adoration, attraction, caring, compassion, fondness, liking, love, sentimentality, tenderness, longing, lust, arousal, desire, infatuation, passion

Sadness

Sadness is a primary emotion.

Definition of Sadness:
An emotional pain associated with, or characterized by, feelings of disadvantage, loss, despair, grief, helplessness, disappointment and sorrow. An individual experiencing sadness may become quiet or lethargic and withdraw themselves from others.

Secondary Emotions to Sadness:
Disappointment, dismay, displeasure, neglect, alienation, defeat, dejection, embarrassment, homesickness, humiliation, insecurity, isolation, insult, loneliness, rejection, depression, despair, gloom, glumness, grief, hopelessness, melancholy, misery, sorrow, unhappiness, woe, shame, guilt, regret, remorse, suffering, agony, anguish, hurt, sympathy, pity

Surprise

Surprise is a primary emotion.

Definition of Suprise:
To strike with wonder or amazement especially because of something unexpected.

Secondary Emotions to Surprise:
Amazement, astonishment

How to Feel Your Emotions

Here is a step-by-step formula for feeling through your emotions

1) An uncomfortable emotion comes up, and your mind starts to create meaning/stories around the emotion (for example: I'm unlovable, I'm in danger of losing xyz, I'm not good enough, I will never achieve xyz, I'm such a loser, worst-case scenario, etc.)

2) Stop - You not actually "feeling" your emotions. You are "thinking" about the ideas you've attached to your emotions. We need to focus on the "feeling" only.

3) Change your awareness and focus on your physical body.

4) Scan your body and locate where you feel the emotion.

5) Describe how the emotion feels inside your body as best you can (is it a shape, color, temperature, texture, sensations, images, sounds, taste etc.)

6) Take a deep breath.

7) Observe the emotion and allow it to simply be there as it is. Notice if the emotion stays the same, moves around, changes, gets more intense or less intense etc. keep breathing into it and observing it.

8) Name the emotion: A quick and short name (anger, sadness, fear etc.)

9) Sometimes the emotion moves from one body part to another. Keep tracking and observing it.

10) Your mind will want to start thinking again and attaching stories and meanings to this emotion. Stop your mind as many times as you need to and keep redirecting your awareness into the sensations inside your body.

11) Notice that although this emotion (this feeling in your body) is uncomfortable, you are still alive, and you have survived.

12) Repeat until you feel the emotion has disappeared or you have a sense of relief or completion.

If you are becoming fatigued due to the intensity and time spent with an uncomfortable emotion you can try temporarily changing your focus to a different body part that feels neutral or good and focus on those sensations for a few seconds. Then switch back to the uncomfortable emotion in the body and continue the exercise.

Example of How to Feel Your Emotions

- I'm noticing a dark, cold ball in between my chest and stomach. It feels like it has spikes.
- It feels like it's made of metal. It kind of tastes like metal too.
- It's getting heavier and I feel pressure in my chest.
- I feel it getting stronger and bigger.
- It feels very uncomfortable. It's getting darker.
- Now I feel a falling sensation.
- The falling sensation is getting more and more uncomfortable.
- It feels almost unbearable but I'm reminding myself that I'm alive.
- It's getting smaller and less intense now.
- It got bigger again, and the falling sensation got faster and stronger.
- I feel scared. This is fear.
- Now the sensations have moved to my thighs.
- The uncomfortable sensation in my thighs feels like a running away sensation. I have the urge to run away.

- Now I feel it in both in my thighs and in my solar plexus but it's stronger in my thighs.
- Now it moved to my arms, and now it feels hot and burning.
- Now it's getting weaker and softer.
- I feel very tired.
- I feel like it's gone now.
- I survived.

Vocabulary for Physical Sensations

Here are some common words used to describe physical sensations associated with emotions.

Learning to feel and describe the emotions in your body (interoception) is a highly evolved skill that takes time and practice. While there are some common sensations and descriptions associated with certain emotions; everyone is unique, and you may feel sensations that are not on this list or that are categorized differently from this list.

Anger
Burning, clenched, constricted, dense, energized, explosive, fiery, hot, knotted, hot, rush, flushed, itchy, jagged, jittery, jumbly, jumpy, knotted, full, goopy, sticky, red, pointy, sharp, heavy, slippery, cloudy, bumpy, grainy

Fear
Cold, dark, shaky, shivery, sweaty, trembling, dizzy, fluttery, nauseous, pit in stomach, queasy, spacey, tingling twitchy, constricted, armored, blocked, clenched, closed, congested, knotted, numb, stuck, suffocated, tense, thick, throbbing, tight, wooden, bloated, breathless, frozen, contracted, goose bumpy, damp, dense, dizzy, icy, wobbly, sharp, pressure, paralyzed, pounding, rolling, black, purple, red

Joy
Activated, breathless, bubbly, buzzy, electric, energized, floating, fluid, radiating, shimmer, tingling, twitchy, open-hearted, airy, alive, awake, expanded, flowing, full, open, relaxed, releasing, smooth spacious, still vital, cool expanding, light, loose silky, smooth, soft, spacious, yellow, purple, green, orange

Love
Soft, aglow, cozy, melting, moved, touched, warm, expanding, shimmering, radiating, hot

Sadness
Disappearing, disconnected, empty, frozen, heavy, hiding, icy, imploding small, achy, bruised, cutting open, piercing, prickly, raw, searing, sensitive ,sore, wobbly, heavy, alone,

down, hole, hollow, untethered, weighted, brittle, chilled, clammy, closed, cold, congested, constricted, crampy, dull, empty, ragged, raw, blue, black, grey

Surprise
Elastic, electric, faint, fluid, flutter, frantic, hot, cold, red, tingly, icy, falling, yellow, rushing

Closing Thoughts

A special note from the author.

Developing psychological flexibility and feeling your emotions is much easier said than done. It takes time and practice to master these skills. The Happy Brain Journal is like a personal trainer for your brain and nervous system. Some days, feeling your emotions may feel like you just ran a marathon. This is within the spectrum of normal. Our mind and body are intricately connected, and our emotions cause real physical sensations and take up energy just like running a marathon or an intense gym session would .

Think about all the most important and meaningful accomplishments you've had so far. They most likely took time and a significant amount of effort. They also probably continue to take time and some effort to maintain.

My hope for you is that with practice, you will become a master at psychological flexibility and this skill will trickle down to all the most important areas of your life, helping you reach your wildest and happiest dreams. You deserve to live a life that is full and rewarding.

I also hope that as each person on this planet becomes more skilled and aware of their internal landscape, our external landscape (mother nature) can heal and thrive so that many generations after us can live on continuing our legacies.

With love,

Esma

Resources

National Institute of Mental Health (nami.org) – A government funded organization that provides educational programs, resources, advocacy, and raises awareness on various mental health conditions.

Suicide Stop (sucidestop.com) – A suicide and self-harm resource center for online chats, worldwide hotlines and emergency numbers, interactive media, useful information and helpful tips.

National Domestic Violence Hotline (thehotline.org) – An organization that provides free, confidential, and compassionate support, crisis intervention information, education, and referral services in over 200 languages.

YOUR SUPPORT MAKES A BIG DIFFERENCE!

When you support our business, you're supporting a dream coming to life.

Share a picture or video of your Happy Brain Journal on social media for **20% OFF your next purchase!**

Email hello@quantummindframe.com with your social media post link to receive your special discount.

Let's connect!

Follow our @quantummindframe social channels.

www.ingramcontent.com/pod-product-compliance
Lightning Source LLC
Chambersburg PA
CBHW072152070526
44585CB00015B/1112